CREWEL
EMBROIDERY

MW00813742

'A fairy tale is but a fairy tale;
whenever you decide to pay no attention to it
it only steps back,
and your life again becomes as ordinary as
a tram.'

Kir Bulychov, a popular science fiction writer when I
was a child.

CREWEL
EMBROIDERY

Tatiana Popova

7 enchanting designs
inspired by fairy tales

SEARCH PRESS

First published by Search Press, 2020

Search Press Limited,
Wellwood, North Farm Road,
Tunbridge Wells, Kent TN2 3DR

Text copyright © Tatiana Popova, 2020

Photographs by Alex Popov and Tatiana Popova

Design copyright © Search Press Ltd 2020

All rights reserved. No part of this book, text,
photographs or illustrations may be reproduced or
transmitted in any form or by any means by print,
photoprint, microfilm, microfiche, photocopier, internet
or in any way known or as yet unknown, or stored
in a retrieval system, without written permission
obtained beforehand from Search Press.

ISBN: 978-1-78221-722-0

The Publishers and author can accept no responsibility
for any consequences arising from the information,
advice or instructions given in this publication.
Readers are permitted to reproduce any of the items/
patterns in this book for their personal use, or for
the purposes of selling for charity, free of charge and
without the prior permission of the Publishers.
Any use of the items/patterns for commercial purposes
is not permitted without the prior permission of
the Publishers.

Suppliers
If you have difficulty in obtaining any of the materials
and equipment mentioned in this book, then please
visit the Search Press website for details of suppliers:
www.searchpress.com

Alternatively, the author provides her own mail-order
service via her website: www.owl-crafts.com

Printed in China

Acknowledgements

To Hazel Blomkamp. I will never stop thanking Providence that
you came to Kiev in 2012 together with Di Van Niekerk!
This is just more proof that you never know what surprising
twists may come out of a casual meeting. Your idea to
replace crewel wool with cotton threads along with your
artistic embroidery masterpieces left me itching to try crewel
embroidery myself – along with your teasing: 'Which is more
beautiful, crewel or ribbonwork?'

To the whole Search Press team and Sophie Kersey, my nice
editor in particular. I'm a perfect lesson in patience, aren't I?
I just wonder how often you thought of
Bernard Shaw's Eliza Doolittle!

To my school Handicraft teacher. You were the Number One
Stitching Lady for me in my school years. Just amazing how you
managed to cope with the lack of craft supplies and embroidery
books, a common problem at that time! You were the first
person to show me books by Search Press, though none of us
knew that this was only the beginning of the story...

To my dearest Father. Thank you for your constant
help and kind support, along with your mild hints
to encourage my perfectionism! I'm not sure
whether I managed to master any of your
lessons on modesty...

To my Granny. Even my Mom got envious
seeing how patient you were, calmly making
me re-do a stitch over and over again. Thank
you for your loving hands and
kind heart – I miss you!

To my wonderful students: we went through
my teaching and stitching experiments
together, witnessing the birth of so many
embroidery wonders, and enjoying it all
very much! This is what I appreciate and
thank you for!

Contents

Introduction

This is a book of fairy tales

I have been fond of stitching since childhood, but I finally decided to become a floristry designer in my teens. This dream failed to come true, but life is so full of twists and turns! Eventually I found the art of silk ribbon embroidery and started creating unfading flower bouquets. At the same time I rediscovered my childish love for intricate embroidery techniques and chose the crewel technique as the best means to express it. And this is the result!

Now every child knows that the one true mark of a good fairy tale book is pictures: plenty of them, colourful, big and bright! It's as easy as pie: the more pictures and the less text a fairy tale book contains, the better. That's why this book consists mainly of pictures, with as little text as possible.

During my years of teaching I have been assured hundreds of times that most of us prefer seeing rather than reading embroidery instructions. Therefore in this book I replace text with images and diagrams wherever possible.

Besides, I want to devote this book to those folk tales and stories which – I believe – played a crucial role in my upbringing. Even as a grown-up, I still love these fairy tales and want to do some stitching in their honour.

This is a book about our lives

Our lives often make the best fairy tales, and stitching is often connected to life events and not only to significant ones, as when we work a birthday present or embroider a Christening dress. Everyday experiences of amazing colours, trips to new places, and enjoyable meetings are often our best source of inspiration. And since embroidery has such a soothing effect, it is always nice to do some thinking while you do it.

Indians have a wonderful custom of commemorating significant moments in their lives by filling small bags with rice and adding a special aroma mix. Every time they want to remind themselves of that moment, they open the bag and smell its aroma. A similar thing often happens to stitching, with certain pieces reminding me: 'Ah, I was embroidering this when my little Mag was a baby!'

This is an embroidery book after all!

When I picked up my embroidery hobby after sleepless nights nursing my babies, I could only follow instructions in books. Alex, my husband, always frowned on this, saying that one day I would develop designs of my own. To tell you the truth, I often lost my temper when he said this – it sounded like teasing, since it was so obviously impossible! That's what I really believed, and I still I have no idea when I finally had my 'aha' moment. Things started changing and about ten years ago I designed my first embroidery kit.

This helped me understand one very important thing: you know literally nothing about your creativity until you try it! I have written this book to give my dear readers the chance to enjoy their own embroidery adventures.

Materials and tools

My style of crewel stitching is a modern variation of traditional Jacobean embroidery. I never use crewel wool or linen twill. This makes it much easier to find the materials for the designs in this book: there is no need to stick to the letter of the 'You will need' lists. Change what you like and use your thread leftovers to create new masterpieces!

FABRICS

I love the look of a smooth surface for stitching, so I prefer to use fine cotton fabrics with some backing to provide solid grounds for my embroidery. I often use off-white or pastel colour fabrics, sometimes experimenting with patterned ones. Silk fabrics are also gorgeous – note that it is helpful to attach a piece of water soluble fleece as a backing. When you have finished stitching, immerse the embroidery in cold water to dissolve the backing. This provides support while you work and keeps the silk fine and delicate for the end result.

THREADS

I usually use DMC threads: solid and variegated stranded cotton and pearl cotton size 8 and 12. Appleton wool would also work! Use your own stock of threads or follow the conversion chart below, showing DMC stranded cotton and pearl cotton threads converted to Appleton crewel wool. If you decide to stitch in Appleton, bear in mind that for some of the areas you might need more or fewer strands than stated. Have a try on a doodle cloth first to see whether you are happy with the result.

DMC TO APPLETON CONVERSION CHART

DMC	APPLETON	DMC	APPLETON	DMC	APPLETON	DMC	APPLETON	DMC	APPLETON
B5200	991b	502	155	733	242	822	791a	3045	343
Ecru	988	503	643	738	762	828	562	3053	154
208	894	517	566	739	761	830	336	3078	872
211	891	518	565	741	476	841	931	3345	256
225	621	519	462	742	475	842	982	3346	426
309	227	522	965	743	694	890	835	3348	401
311	326	554	451	744	842	902	716	3705	502
315	528	561	157	745	851	913	524	3753	561
320	644	640	967	746	881	931	323	3756	991b
351	124	642	965	760	143	938	338	3760	486
352	204	646	966	761	753	945	762	3765	489
353	622	647	924	772	847	959	463	3787	968
368	402	666	995	778	711	987	403	3813	524
369	541	676	902	794	821	988	424	3822	902
415	963	712	881	814	716	989	402	3823	331a
444	312	725	312	815	305	3022	965	3842	488
501	156	727	842	816	148	3033	971	3865	991b

NEEDLES

Use a size 10 embroidery needle for silk shading and size 22 and 24 or 26 tapestry needles for weaving, needlelace techniques or stitches where it is important not to go through the thread of a finished stitch. Use size 24 and 26 chenille needles for all the other stitches.

EMBROIDERY FRAMES AND HOOPS

I prefer embroidery frames. I use R & R Universal Craft frames made in the UK. Q-snaps are the equivalent, produced in the USA. You can use your favourite small round hoops or similiar: the only important thing is to keep the fabric taut.

If a design includes silk shading, or if it is big and you want to see the whole stitching area at once, a slate frame is the best choice, as it provides drum-tight tension and the fabric doesn't loosen. You will find instructions for dressing a slate frame in embroidery books and online. You can also use stretcher bars if you prefer them, as well as scroll frames, sometimes called lap frames.

It is often a good idea to use backing fabric along with the design fabric. The question is how to stretch both of them evenly and tightly. Some frames (like R & R or Millennium frames) allow you to fix both layers simultaneously like one piece of heavier fabric.

But for most frames you have to stretch one layer first and then attach the other one on top or underneath. I prefer to stretch the design fabric, then add the backing fabric underneath it using running stitch. Some influential embroidery schools recommend stretching the backing first, then placing the design fabric on top of it, fixing it with herringbone stitch. Whichever way you choose, it is important to stretch the first fabric so that it can flex: it should be firm but not drum tight. When the second fabric is applied, tension both layers at the same time.

TRACING DESIGNS

For my own stitching I prefer using a plain HB pencil, as it draw fine, faint lines which can easily be covered with stitches. In my crewel sets, I use fine Micron pens because they make brighter and longer-lasting lines.

Pre-shrink the fabric and iron it before you start transferring designs. Use a light box for middleweight fabrics, but you might not need this for fine and delicate fabrics. Just put a pattern underneath those fabrics on a table or any hard, flat surface to trace it.

PINCUSHIONS

These are such little things, but I love them! My own pincushion is like a huge needle park containing needles for every occasion, as well as scissors, fabric markers, etc. This is the permanent home for my needles.

For temporary safekeeping I use a tiny jam jar with a magnet attached under the lid. I just drop my middle-size needles onto the lid.

For the finest needles I have a tiny thimble 'vase', which ends up looking like a needle bouquet. I like to use a needle minder – a very handy device. I also love to make funny pincushions, like the ones made of pompons.

Compare the design lines worked in HB pencil and Micron pen.

Be creative

In early childhood, long before I found the joy of playing with dolls, my favourite toys were mosaics, colouring books and the magic tube of a kaleidoscope.

I treated colouring in as a job: I was sure all those line drawings badly needed some colour and I had to help them. It never ceased to amaze me how the impression created by a picture could be changed dramatically by applying a different colour. This became especially obvious when colouring story books where the same character appeared again and again: changing the colour palette produced completely different moods.

The plain-looking tube of my kaleidoscope seemed to be a universe containing numerous bright, patterned worlds. It seemed unbelievable that all those totally different patterns were generated from same set of small beads! It was completely wonderful to me, especially when my Daddy explained that less than one-third of the whole design was really there – all the rest was its reflection in three mirrors.

But my mosaic board was best of all. I could play with it all day long and had no doubt it was going to be my favourite toy for the rest of my life! With mosaics you do not need to be an artist to draw things: you create pictures with tiles. And whatever imperfections my designs had, I knew it was due to the limited options of the mosaic board and not my own lack of skill. This gave me great confidence. Moreover, having developed a certain pattern, I could do it repeatedly, using different colours to make the same designs.

Believe it or not, these childish games gave me ideas for this book. The first was to divide the outlines of the book's largest design, Tree of Happiness, into parts, and

Changing the colour palette produced completely different moods

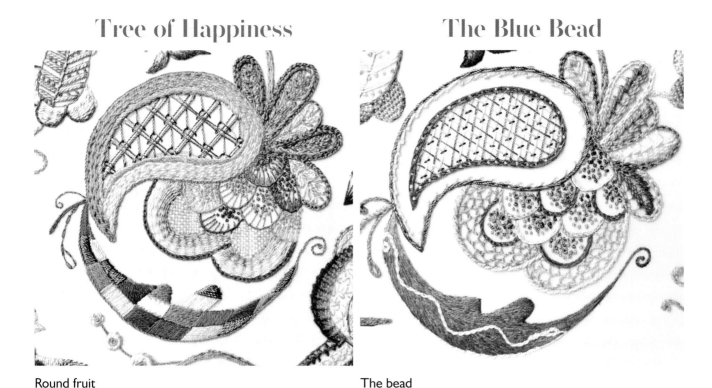

Tree of Happiness

Round fruit

Stitching instructions, page 64.

The Blue Bead

The bead

Stitching instructions, page 84.

then reassemble them in a new way to create the many smaller designs featured. This is like getting new designs from the same set of beads in a kaleidoscope. Secondly I decided to give a different look to the same pattern by working it in different stitches and colours – creating variations on a theme, just as in my mosaics and colouring books. Thus every element of Tree of Happiness has been embroidered at least twice. And look at the results – compare the images below.

Tree of Happiness

The Blue Bead

Pointed leaf

Stitching instructions, page 62.

Pointed leaf

Stitching instructions, page 88.

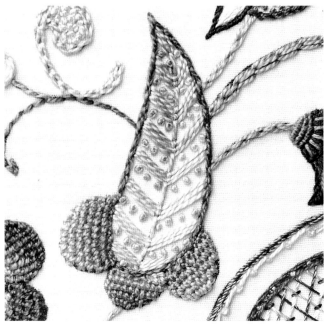

Pepper

Stitching instructions, page 62.

Pepper

Stitching instructions, page 90.

Tree of Happiness

Emerald City

Crowned flower

Stitching instructions, page 60.

Crowned flower

Stitching instructions, pages 99, 100 and 101.

Scalloped leaf

Stitching instructions, page 70.

Scalloped leaf

Stitching instructions, page 102.

Tree of Happiness

Fruit capsules

Stitching instructions, page 66.

Bluebell

Stitching instructions, page 70.

Fire-bud

Stitching instructions, page 78.

Scarlet Sails

Fruit capsules

Stitching instructions, page 125.

Tulip

Stitching instructions, page 122.

Red fire-bud and Dotted fire-bud

Stitching instructions, pages 120 and 122.

Tree of Happiness

Crewel Waltz

Dancing flower

Stitching instructions, page 76.

Dancing flower

Stitching instructions, page 132.

Tree of Happiness

Elisa

Pumpkin

Stitching instructions, page 66.

Flower

Stitching instructions, page110.

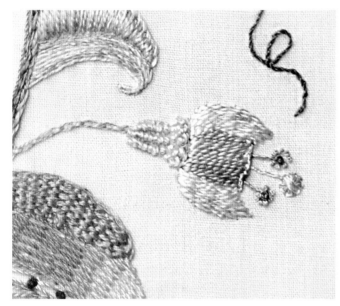

Bluebell

Stitching instructions, page 66.

Bluebell

Stitching instructions, page 113.

Textured bluebells

Stitching instructions, page 114.

Stitch world

I admit that my passion for using a huge variety of stitches for my designs has long become an obsession. In this chapter you will find 100 (!) embroidery stitches and techniques, all featured in the designs in this book. In the wider universe of stitches, this is my very own stitch world.

Most of these stitches are classical ones and well known all around the globe. Just a few are my own interpretation, shared from my personal stitching experience.

A picture is worth a thousand words! Since most of us are visual learners, this chapter consists mostly of photographs and diagrams, with a very brief description where necessary. A couple of intricate stitches need more explanation; those are featured on separate pages along with tips and step-by-step images.

A picture is worth a thousand words – most of us are visual learners

I have used a few simple symbols for the stitch guide, and some diagrams are colour-coded to show the order of stitching. Please look carefully through the following notes before you start working.

Diagrams and photographs

You will find a few special symbols in the diagrams and in some of the photographs. They are there to facilitate the explanation. Please keep their meaning in mind.

RAINBOW COLOURS

As everybody knows, a primary rainbow shows a spectrum of colours in the following order: red, orange, yellow, green, blue, indigo and violet. The sequence of work for some stitches in this chapter is shown in that of rainbow colours. It means that a stitch marked in red should be performed first, then comes the one in orange, followed by the one in yellow, and so on. See the example for Basket stitch below.

SEQUENCE OF WORK FOR BASKET STITCH

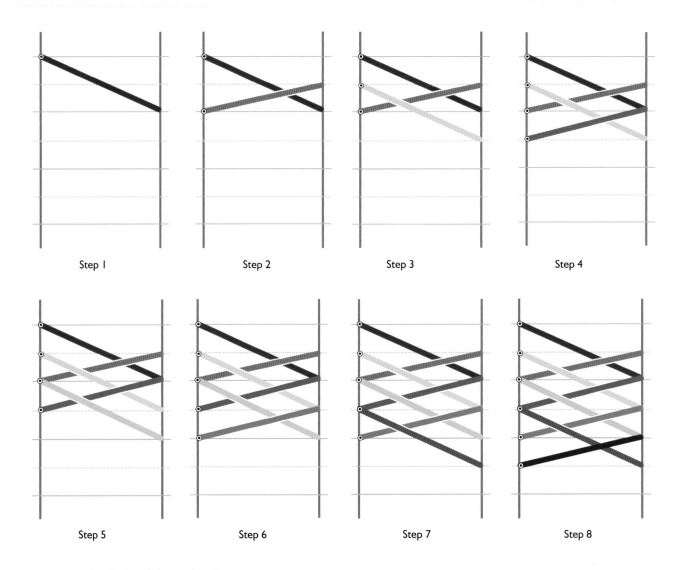

Step 1　　　　Step 2　　　　Step 3　　　　Step 4

Step 5　　　　Step 6　　　　Step 7　　　　Step 8

BLACK DOTS

A black dot symbol on a stitch indicates its starting point – the place where you come up with your needle, as shown here.

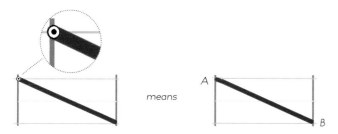

BLACK ARROWS

A black arrow next to the needle in some of the photographs indicates the direction of needle movement.

THREAD COLOUR AND TEXTURE

Now and then the photographs show a stitch worked in thread of two or three contrasting colours. This is just for clarity in the demonstrations, but you are not meant to use all these colours of course. Work using just one colour of thread as usual.

In some of the photographs, you will see hairy-looking thread, even though the 'You will need' list includes no woollen thread. This is because cotton thread was often replaced with tapestry wool for the demonstration photographs, to make them clearer.

RIGHT- OR LEFT-HANDER

All the stitches in this chapter were performed by right-handed embroiderers. If you are a left-handed stitcher, work them in mirror image. Note that sometimes it is really helpful to use an actual mirror for this!

SEWING VS STABBING

They are the two ways of stitching. Using the sewing method, you come up and down through the fabric in one movement of your needle. This is a quick way of embroidering, but it is not as precise as the stabbing method. Stabbing is a better method for most embroidery designs, as it gives a neater result. This means coming up with one movement of your needle and going down in another.

If you are using a small embroidery hoop and you feel confident with the stitches, the sewing method is better, as it speeds up your work. I prefer stabbing, but don't be surprised that the sewing method often appears in the stitch photographs. This was done for two reasons: it provides a better needle position for photographs, and it helps reduce the number of pictures needed to demonstrate a stitch. However, when it comes to practice, I vote for the stabbing method every time!

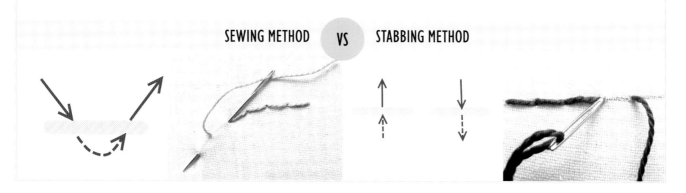

SEWING METHOD **VS** STABBING METHOD

Stitch index

The stitches in this chapter are in alphabetic order and so is the Stitch index on pages 158–159. Use the Stitch index as a handy tool to help you find a particular stitch instruction quickly.

To knot or not to knot?

The question every embroiderer faces when starting a new project: is it OK to knot the thread tail at the beginning of a new line of stitching, or should you use some laborious technique to avoid this? In the 19th century, this was a question of life or death for professional embroiderers: if their work was not wanted due to its 'poor quality', they got no payment. Nowadays things are different, and my policy is to avoid knots for needlepoint, silk shading and other techniques where the back of the work should look good, but to knot the thread for other stitches. There is one 'but' of course: tie a knot if it will not interfere with your filling stitches or with the ultimate purpose of the embroidery – for instance, if you are stitching a silk blouse, you don't want knots on the reverse side.

Stitch names

It's no secret that most embroidery stitches are known by at least two names. This happens for different reasons, geography being one of them. For example, one of the traditional Ukrainian stitches used for embroidering towels is called Poltava (or Poltavian) stitch in my country, Ukraine, but it is known internationally as Romanian stitch. Another example is Bayeux stitch, a well-known ancient stitch used in crewel work. In Ukraine, it is called Eastern stitch and it is used mostly for ecclesiastical embroidery.

If I were writting an embroidery dictionary, it would be correct to mention all the possible names for one stitch. However, this is not the best idea for an instruction book, which needs to convey practical information. Therefore, I have tried to use the most popular of the stitch names, except for a few cases in which two names for a stitch are well known. In these cases, I give both names.

Stitch geography

It never ceases to amaze me how international the art of embroidery is. The stitches in this book have names originating in quite a number of countries, cities, and towns: Germany, Hungary, Romania, Portugal, the island of Rhodes in Greece; Bokhara, Brussels, Bayeux and Mountmellick, the Irish town which we might never have heard of were it not for the stitch named after it.

Stitch relatives

You may have noticed that thread couching, if worked in several rows placed close together, develops into Bokhara stitch, and if the couched thread meanders around the area, it forms Vermicelli stitch. Work thread couching on top of Satin stitch and you end up with Bayeux stitch.

Note comparisons between stitches – what's similar and what's different – and you'll learn them all in no time!

ALTERNATE STEM STITCH

BACKSTITCH

BASKET STITCH

The stitches in the photographs are spaced out for clarity. Work them closer together.

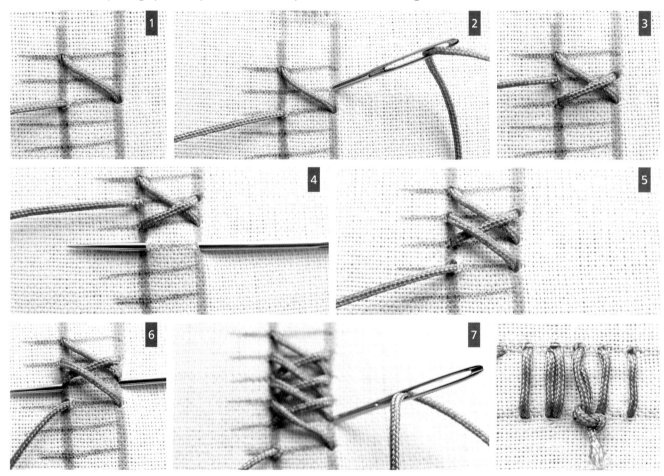

The back.

BATTLEMENT COUCHING

Work 3 to 5 layers of lattice, placing them on top of each other with a small shift. Couch the top layer only.

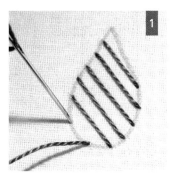 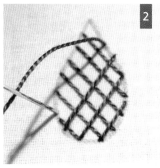

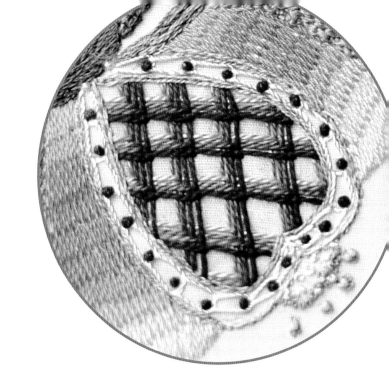

BAYEUX STITCH

The back.

The single-colour stitch variation (shown at the top of the shape in blue) is classical.

BLANKET STITCH

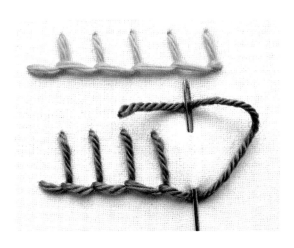

BOKHARA COUCHING

There are various options for the placing of couching stitches:

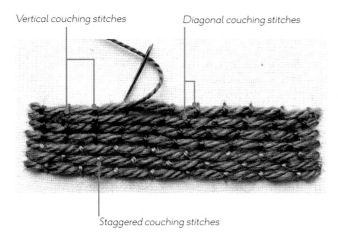

Vertical couching stitches

Diagonal couching stitches

Staggered couching stitches

BRUSSELS STITCH, 3 + 1

(a.k.a. Detached buttonhole stitch, 3 + 1)
See more tips on the opposite page. Work a group of three Detached buttonhole stitches, then add one more stitch under the group (shown in indigo and lilac arrows).

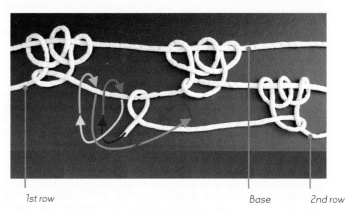

1st row   *Base*   *2nd row*

BULLION KNOT

See the images opposite.
Step 1: Note the position of the needle!
Step 2: Work as many wraps around the needle tip as needed so that the length of the wrapped part is equal to the length of the space marked B–C. Gently pull the needle through the wraps. The result is shown in the inset photograph.
Step 3: Couch down the finished Bullion knot.

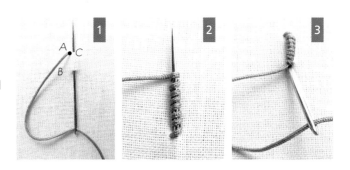

BURDEN STITCH

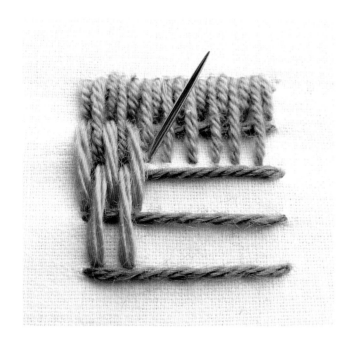

BURDEN STITCH 2

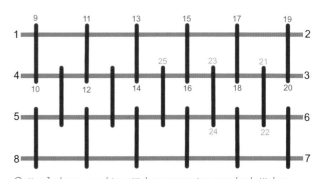

Option 1, above: couching stitches go over two couched stitches.

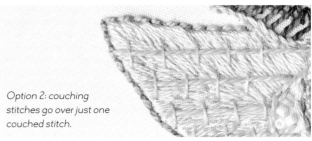

Option 2: couching stitches go over just one couched stitch.

NEEDLELACE: BRUSSELS STITCH

(a.k.a. Detached buttonhole stitch)
In fact, this is not just one stitch. It has numerous variations, known as the needlelace technique. Variations of needlelace are perfectly developed in Romanian, Armenian and Irish lace. Most countries in Western Europe are familiar with Brussels lace, which gave this stitch its name.

You will find four variations of Brussels stitch used to embroider the designs in this book, but of course there are a lot more. The variations used for this book are shown opposite.

Double Brussels stitch.

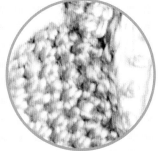

Corded single Brussels stitch.

note:

See my own personal experience of Brussels stitch on page 81. It will make you smile.

Although Ceylon stitch is not usually considered part of the needlelace group, it is similar in many ways, so you will find this information useful for this stitch as well.

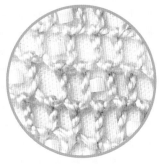

Twisted Brussels stitch (aka. tulle bars).

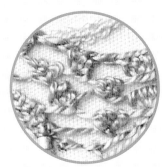

Brussels stitch, 3+1.

All the Brussels stitches share the same method for starting, proceeding with and finishing.

STARTING

The three most popular ways are to work Backstitch, a line of Thread couching or Chain stitch (as shown in the images). I find Backstitch works well for a curved line, Thread couching is good for a straight line (if the stitch area has any) and Chain stitch is shown for Ceylon stitch on page 26. Always try to choose the longest and least curved side of the area as your starting point (see the diagram, right).

Backstitch.

Thread couching.

Where to start.

Chain stitch.

PROCEEDING

Follow the specific diagram for each kind of Brussels stitch. To start and finish each row, use any of the two options described below. The first is my favourite, but the second is considered classical.
a) Come up at the beginning of a row and go down to the back of the fabric at the end.
b) Work Backstitch along the edges and intertwine the working thread. Whichever option you choose, it is important to consider the width of a row in the kind of Brussels stitch you are working. Then you will be able to move down the right distance to start a new row.

Option a.

Option b.

FINISHING

Again, either couch the last row of Brussels stitch or intertwine it with the Backstitch line worked at the bottom. I vote for the first option again, though the second one is more common.

Every kind of Brussels stitch looks better outlined. To do this, use any kind of line stitch: Stem stitch, Rope stitch, Chain stitch, Whipped backstitch etc.

Working option a.

Working option b.

BUTTONHOLE SCALLOPS

tip

You may find it easier to work a Straight stitch first (shown in yellow thread).

BUTTONHOLE STITCH

BUTTONHOLE WHEEL

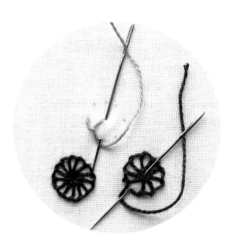

CEYLON STITCH

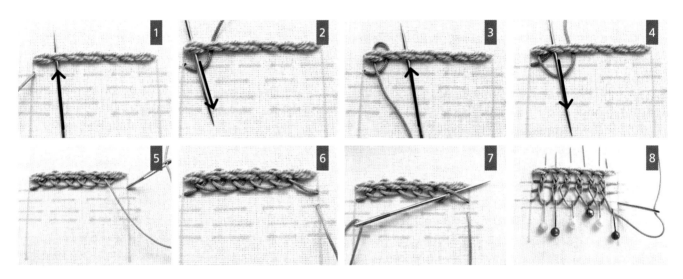

CHAIN STITCH

CORAL STITCH

CORDED SINGLE BRUSSELS STITCH

a.k.a. Corded detached buttonhole stitch

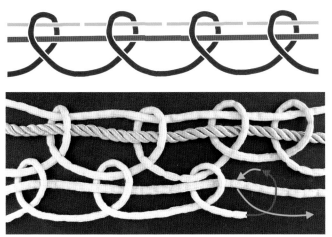

COUCHING

A) SEED BEADS

B) THREAD

CRETAN STITCH

Cretan stitch.

Feather stitch.

Think of Cretan stitch as a wider and shallower variation of Feather stitch.

Note that lines B and C may be placed either closer or further apart from lines A and D. This is how the stitch gets its numerous variations.

The stitches in these photographs are spaced for clarity, but you should work them closer together.

DOUBLE BRUSSELS STITCH

See page 25 for more tips. The black arrows (bottom diagram) mark the beginning of each row.

DOUBLE-THREADED BACKSTITCH

Use thread of the same or a contrasting colour.

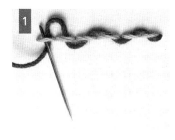

DOUBLE LATTICE + 4-STITCH COUCHING

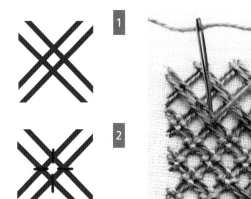

FEATHER STITCH

FERN STITCH

Start each stitch at the black dot. See page 18 for the key to the diagram.

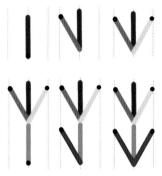

FLY STITCH

FLY STITCH LEAF

Work a number of Fly stitches close together to fill a leaf shape.

FRENCH KNOT

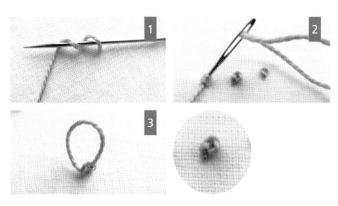

FANCY FILLING STITCH

This stitch is a free-form interpretation of quite a number of weaving techniques and filling stitches. The thread choice featured here is just one of the numerous options. You can also use your own.

   This stitch was used for the Elisa design, see page 104.

Threads

COTTON PEARL DMC
Size 8 (colours A and B) for step 1
Size 8 (colour C) for step 2
Size 12 (colour D) for step 3

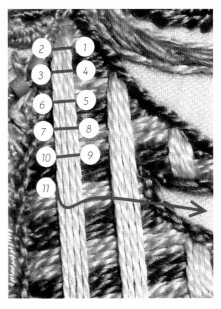

The first layer: Using threads of two contrasting colours (A and B), work groups of four Straight stitches, alternating the thread colour each time you start stitching a new group. Continue until all the area is filled.

The second layer: Change to thread C (the colour option shown here is actually just a lighter tone of thread B to produce a 3D effect). Work groups of four Straight stitches perpendicular to the stitches of the first layer. Be sure to place these groups at equal intervals, each about the same width as the group itself.

Couching: Use thread D. It is important to choose a finer thread for this step compared to steps 1 and 2. Work Straight stitches on top of and across the stitches of the second layer, as shown. Come up at 1, go down to the back of the fabric at 2, up again at 3 etc. Note that this is supposed to be stitching, not weaving: couch the groups of four stitches down onto the fabric. The couching stitches are placed in such a way that they look like the borders of squares. These squares are in fact intersections of the two previous stitch layers.

The finished stitch

As often happens to filling stitches, the stitched area needs outlining with any kind of border stitch, e.g. Stem stitch or Split stitch for a neater look.

GERMAN KNOTTED BUTTONHOLE STITCH

Step 4 is a repeat of Step 1. Continue working Buttonhole stitches in pairs, wrapping each pair with your thread.

HEAVY CHAIN STITCH

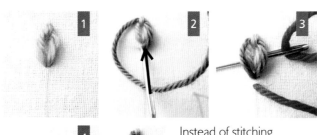

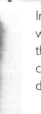

Instead of stitching with one thread, three threads of contrasting colours were used for the demonstrations.

HUNGARIAN BRAIDED CHAIN STITCH

To make each stitch more distinct, threads of three contrasting colours were used. Usually only one is used.

GRANITOS

Bring your needle up at the black dots. The rainbow colour flow shows the sequence of stitching (see page 18). Always go through the same two holes in the fabric. Work a straight stitch first (red), then place the second stitch to the left (orange) and the third one (yellow) to the right of the first stitch. Continue until you are happy with the size of the stitch.

HERRINGBONE STITCH

The work order is shown in rainbow colour flow (see page 18).

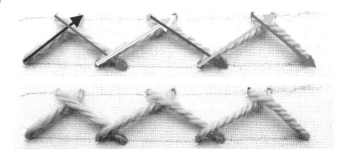

LARK'S HEAD SCALLOPS

A rope is used as a base for the Lark's head knots in the photograph. You should work a loose Lazy daisy stitch as a base for the scallop.

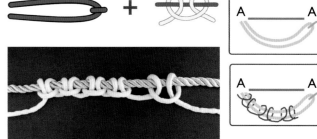

LATTICE (LATTICE FILLING)

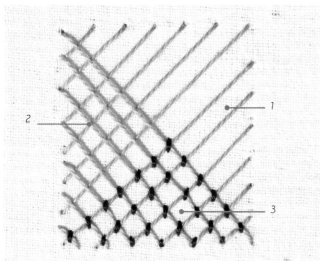

LATTICE + FLY STITCH COUCHING

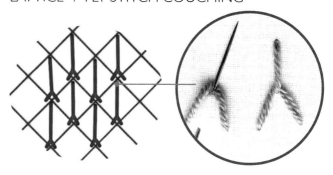

Optional: Work three stitches for each lattice line instead of the usual one. This option is shown below.

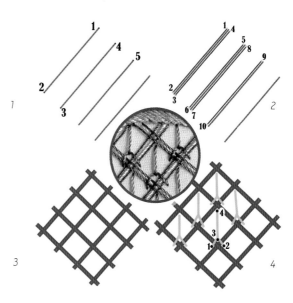

LATTICE + PISTIL STITCH COUCHING

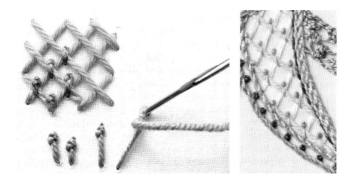

LATTICE + WOVEN FILLING

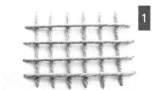 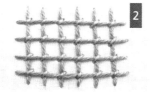 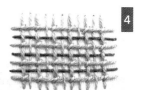

Steps 1 and 2 show Lattice filling.

Step 3: Weave with wrap (green) thread. The pink marks show the order of weaving that looks best to me. Steps 3 and 4 should be worked in the same colour thread.

Step 4: Weave with weft (lilac) thread. Always go under the lattice (blue threads) and over the warp threads (green).

Another option for step 4: Alter the order of weaving for even and odd passings of thread. For the first and all the odd passings, work as it is shown above (under the blue and over the green threads), and for the second and all the even ones, go vice versa (over the blue and under the green threads). This was used for some Blue Bead design areas, although I prefer the first method.

LAZY DAISY STITCH

LAZY TUNING FORK STITCH

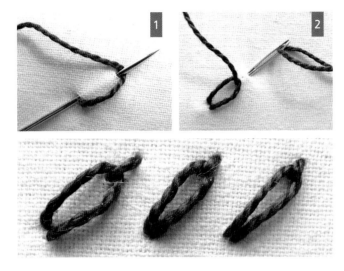

Work a line of Backstitch (step 1) or couched thread. Continue with steps 2 and 3 as shown in yellow thread. Contrasting colours were used for clarity, and this might in fact look nice for some designs.

LOOP STITCH

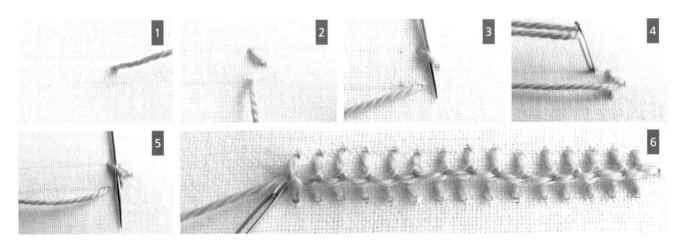

MOUNTMELLICK STITCH

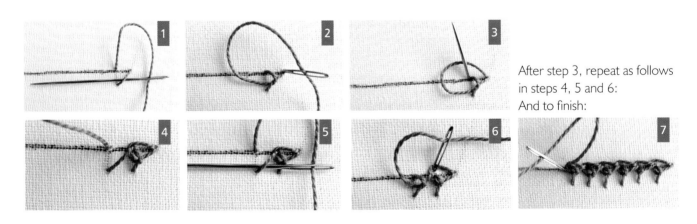

After step 3, repeat as follows in steps 4, 5 and 6:
And to finish:

OPEN CHAIN STITCH

a.k.a. Ladder chain or Square chain
To finish this stitch, work two Stab stitches instead of the usual one (see the red arrows).

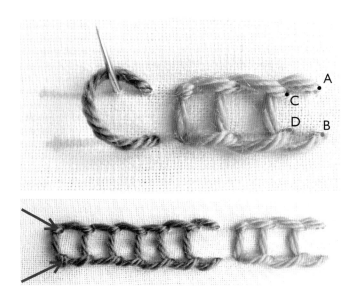

OPEN FISHBONE STITCH

See page 18 for the key to the rainbow colour flow.

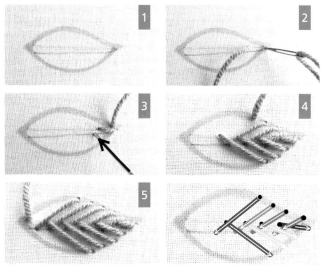

OVERLAPPING BUTTONHOLE STITCH

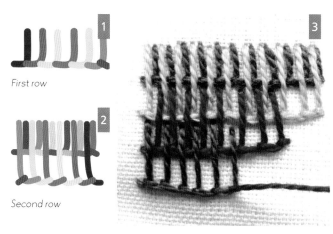

See page 18 for the key to the rainbow colour flow, which shows the sequence of stitching.

First row: Work a line of spaced Buttonhole stitches. The gap between them should be small: just enough to fit one stitch. Also keep in mind that this is the only row in which the stitches are half their normal length.
Second row (overlapping the first): Work full-size stitches, placing them in the gaps in the previous row.
Third row: repeat the first row, but this time make the stitches full-size.

PADDED BUTTONHOLE SCALLOPS

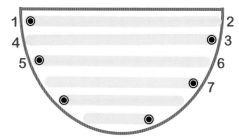

Step 1: Pad a scallop in Satin stitch, using 3 to 6 strands of stranded cotton thread.

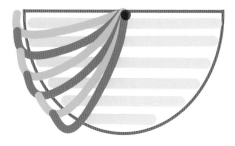

Step 2: Work buttonhole stitch over the padded area, so that the stitches fan out from the centre of the area (see the red dot). This time use just one or two strands of the same thread you used for padding.

PADDED BUTTONHOLE STITCH

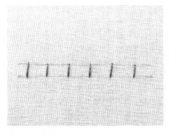

Step1: Make guiding stitches (to be removed later).

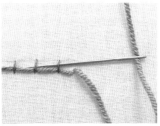

Step 2: Padding (use the same thread as for stitching).

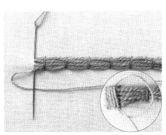

Step 3: Stitch Buttonhole stitches over the padding. Remove a guiding stitch when you approach it with your stitching (see inset).

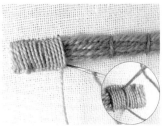

Step 4: Stab stitch to finish. If gaps appear, fill them with a Straight stitch as shown (see inset).

PADDED BUTTONHOLE WITH BULLION PICOTS

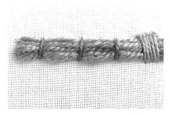

Step 1: Stitch a group of five Buttonhole stitches.

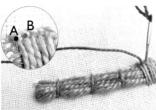

Step 2: Come up at A, then go down at B, leaving a loop on top (A and B being gaps between stitches).

Step 3: Come up at A with the needle just protruding. Work eight wraps round the tip of the needle.

note:

Use the same colour thread for all the steps. The contrasting colours are used here for clarity.

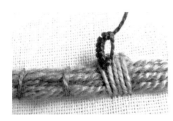

Step 4: Bring the needle through the wraps.

Step 5: Continue working the Buttonhole stitches of the next group, and the Bullion knot will be tightened and shaped.

PADDED RAISED STEM STITCH

Work the padding over the area (step 1). Then do the Raised stem stitch on top of the padding (steps 2 to 6).

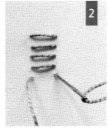
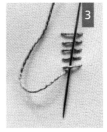
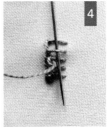

PADDED SATIN STITCH

Threads of contrasting colours are used for clarity. Use one or two threads for stitching and three to six for padding.

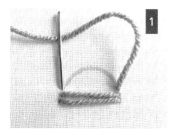   

PALESTRINA STITCH

I prefer working this stitch in an asymmetrical way, which is how it appears in the designs of this book. My variation of the stitch has one side that is flat (along the blue line), and the other side notched.

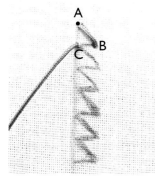 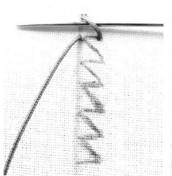  

Step 1: Work a stitch.

Step 2: Go to the left.

Step 3: Go down.

Step 4: Continue in the same way, then on the final stitch, finish as shown.

PICOT STITCH
a.k.a. Woven picot

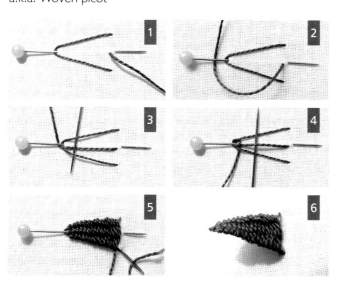

PISTIL STITCH

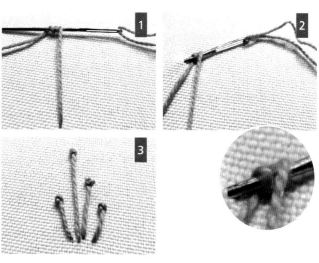

PLAITED BRAID STITCH

See detailed instructions opposite.

PORTUGUESE BORDER STITCH

First work stitches for the base and bring the thread up. Threads of contrasting colours are used here for clarity.

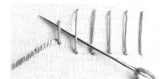

Step 1: Go under two stitches. Repeat three times.

Step 2: Go under just one stitch of the base.

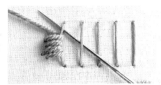

Step 3: Go under two stitches again, but this time just once.

Step 4: Go under one stitch again.

Step 5: Continue in this way. Go down to finish one side of the stitch.

Step 6: Come up for the other side. Stitch the other side then go down to finish.

PORTUGUESE KNOTTED STEM STITCH

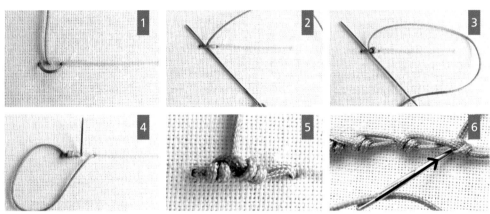

RAISED CHAIN STITCH BAND

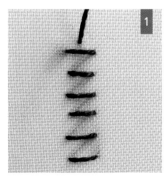
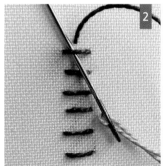
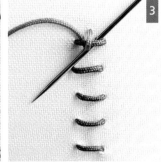

PLAITED BRAID STITCH

This rather tricky stitch is worth trying on a doodle cloth first, using thick thread and a blunt tapestry needle. The basic element consists of three stitches and reminds me of an X intertwined with a smile. The sequence of stitching is shown in the diagram (right) in the rainbow colour flow with black dots marking the beginning of each stitch.

Draw two parallel vertical lines (the grey lines in the diagrams, below). The heavier the thread, the further apart the lines need to be placed. For a stitch sample leave 1cm (½in) between them. Mark the centre (the blue dotted line).

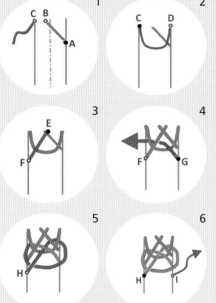

1 2

3 4

5 6

Step 1: Bring your needle up at A. Go down at B (note that this is a little left of centre). Come up at C again. The pink lines in the diagram show the current step, while the green ones are for the previous steps.

Step 2: Bring your needle down through the fabric at D, leaving a loop which looks like a smile!

3 Come up at E, just a little to the right of centre. Go down at F, thus extending the stalk of the letter X. The basic element is finished!

Step 4: Come up at G, level with F. Pass through the loop under the thread intersection, but do not go through the fabric. Tip: leave a loop, do not completely tighten the thread at the interval marked with the blue dots. This keeps the hole in the centre accessible.

Step 5: Place your thread in a smile shape. Now for the trickiest part of the process. Slip your needle under the two stalks (see the white arrows in the photograph below for the second part of step 5). Then through the hole from the previous step. Tighten the thread and go to the back of the fabric at H.

Step 6: Bring your needle up at I. After this, everything is just a repeat.

Photograph of step 4.

First part of step 5.

Second part of step 5. The two white arrows show that the needle slips under TWO 'stalks' that sit on the right-hand vertical guide line.

Step 6. After this, continue as shown in the photographs.

To finish, go to the back of the fabric in the centre of the stitch, level with the two bottom stalks.

The green arrows show that the space between all the stalks is equal.

RAISED CHAIN STITCH BAND + WOVEN FILLING

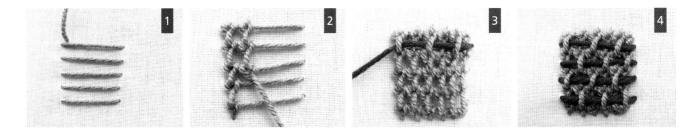

RAISED FISHBONE STITCH LEAF

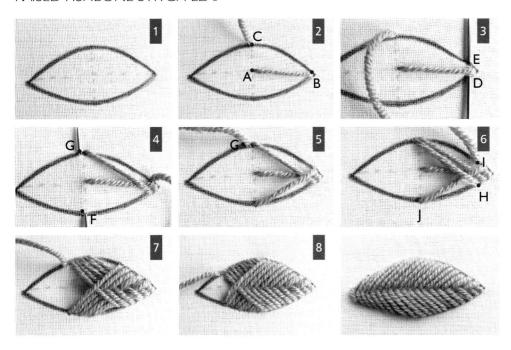

RAISED STEM STITCH

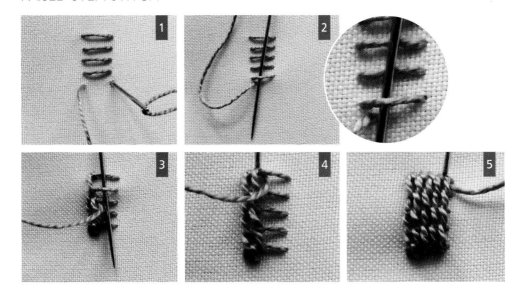

RHODES STITCH

The rainbow colour flow shows the sequence of stitching.

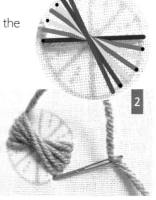

RIBBED FILLING STITCH

Variation of Ribbed spider web stitch

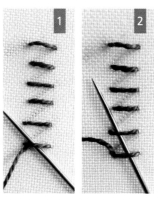

RIBBED SPIDER WEB STITCH

a.k.a. Ribbed wheel, Whipped wheel, Whipped spider wheel, Whipped spider wheel filling

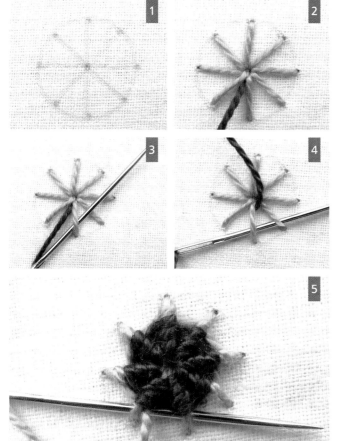

RIBBON ROSE

a.k.a. Rolled ribbon rose

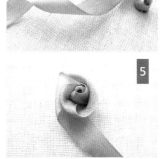

Step 1: Fix both the ribbon tail and the thread in the centre of the rose.
Step 2: Go around the centre to make a kind of ribbon roll.
Step 3: Stab stitch the roll at the bottom.
Step 4: Twist the ribbon tail.
Step 5: Place the twisted ribbon around the rose centre, stab-stitching it here and there as you wish.
Step 6: Go on until the rose is the required size.

ROMANIAN STITCH

ROPE STITCH

The blue line is the design contour. Draw a parallel line close to it. Always come up with your needle on the design line and down on this parallel line. Work a small couching stitch to finish (the black line, bottom right).

RUNNING STITCH

SATIN STITCH

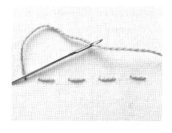

SATIN STITCH BLOCKS

Work square or diamond-shaped blocks, placing satin stitches in neighbouring blocks at right angles to each other. Play around with colour combinations. See page 65 for more tips.

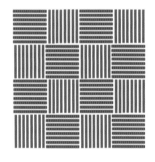

SCALLOPED BUTTONHOLE CHAIN STITCH

I love the variation of this stitch with its scallops overlapping. To create these I go down at A and up at B as shown.

SCROLL STITCH

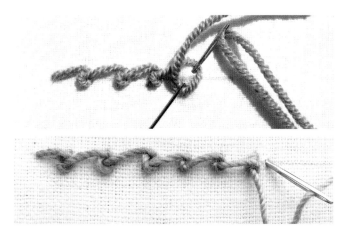

SEED BEADS

(attached separately)

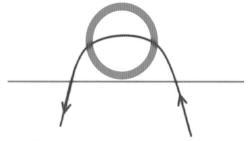

Diagram: a seed bead attached separately.

SEEDING STITCH

This is similar to Backstitch, except that the stitches are smaller and more spaced.

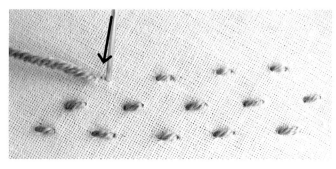

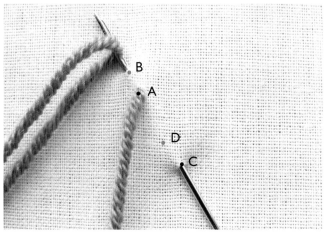

SILK SHADING

a.k.a. Long and short stitch shading
See page 42 for details on preparation for Silk shading. Work in one or two strands of stranded cotton thread. The former option results in far more delicate stitching. The images show stitches of neighbouring zones just touching each other. In fact, you can also split them. Marking the zones (see the blue lines) is very helpful. You can also mark the direction of stitching (see the pink lines). To get a neat outline, work Split stitch along the contour of the area before you start stitching (see page 43). Take the time and patience to practise before starting. This stitch proves that practice makes perfect.

Continued on next page ...

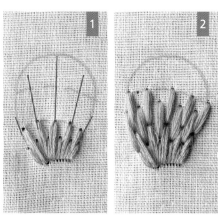

PREPARATION FOR SILK SHADING

Step 1: Divide the area into any number of colour zones: each zone will be worked in its own colour shade. Note that since long and short stitches are to be used, these lines may mark the end of either type.

Step 2: Draw guide lines for the stitches. These lines show the direction in which to place stitches in a particular part of the area. First draw a line in the centre, then divide the halves into quarters and so on. Each time the line should go through the middle of the area.

Step 3: Outlining helps to make the borders of the area smoother and neater. When stitching a detached element, work the outline stitch around the whole perimeter. For joint elements, just outline the outer edge as shown: the bigger leaf is outlined in Chain stitch and the smaller one in the more popular Split stitch.

PREPARING TO STITCH THE TREE OF HAPPINESS

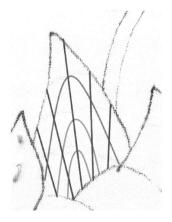 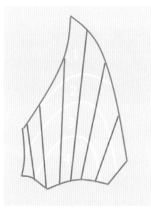 

The colour zones are different shapes. In fact, the shape does not matter much and you can work any you like. Zones 3 and 4 are stitched in thread of the same colour. This is rare in stitch shading, but it is sometimes worth doing: for the Emerald City design, all four zones of the leaves were stitched in the same colour tone.

See how the guide lines match the actual stitching. The question is where to start stitching: I was always told it should be the area marked here as no. 4. Now it seems more popular to start from the outlined zone (no.1). To split or not to split? That is another question. Usually, splitting some stitches from the previous area makes your shading smoother.

tip

The guide lines for stitch direction can be embroidered instead of drawn. I adopted this trick as a pupil learning Silk shading as it is good for impatient embroiderers like me! Just work Straight stitches at equal intervals, embroidering for instance from left to right. Each stitch should be placed in the right direction for the area it is in. Then go from right to left and work stitches in the middle of each interval. Now left to right again, filling in the space in between the stitches. You can also work the first set of stitches, for instance the long ones, altering the length of the others accordingly. This way you will certainly not make the back as perfect as it is in Chinese silk embroideries. Still, it will not spoil the look of the back too much, and if you find this method helpful, I think it is worth trying, especially when taking your first steps in Silk shading. You will know when you are ready to move on to the usual way of stitching. In my view, anything that makes mastering the shading technique less stressful is definitely worth a try.

SPLIT STITCH

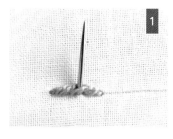   

STEM STITCH

  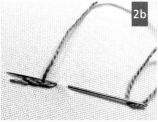

Some resources differentiate between Stem stitch and Outline stitch, depending on the placement of the needle (see options 2a and 2b). In my country and in this book, they are considered the same.

STEM STITCH ROSE

(with knotted centre)
Work Stem stitch around three French knots in the centre.

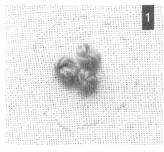 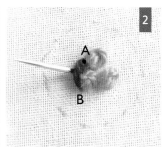

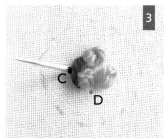 

TUNING FORK STITCH

Start with a Straight stitch, then work Fly stitches close together (see the stitching in blue and red thread in the last image).

The rainbow colour flow shows the sequence of stitching; black dots mark the beginning of each stitch.

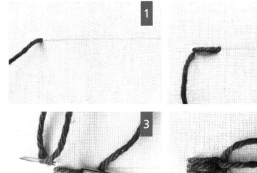

STRAIGHT STITCH

The final stitch.

TWISTED CHAIN STITCH

This stitch is very similar to Rope stitch. The only difference is the space left between the stitches of a chain.

tip

Draw the design line (shown in blue). Draw or imagine a second line (shown dotted). Always come up on the blue line and down at the dotted line.

This is the Twisted chain stitch. Work it repeatedly along the stitch line.

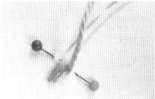

The trick is to make a start for each next stitch at the right point, as shown here.

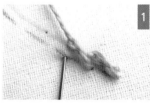

To finish the stitch line, just couch the last loop as shown.

TWISTED CORD

Ribbon is used here to show the twisting. Do the same trick using any number of threads. Fold the twisted thread(s) in half and then let the two halves intertwine with each other. Do not forget to knot the end of the cord, otherwise the cord untwists.

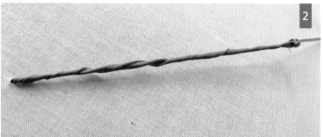

TWISTED SINGLE BRUSSELS STITCH   a.k.a. Twisted buttonhole lace stitch

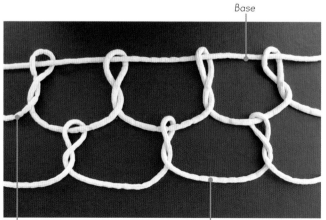

Base

1st row

2nd row

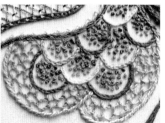

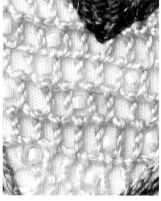

Twisted single Brussels stitch

VAN DYKE STITCH

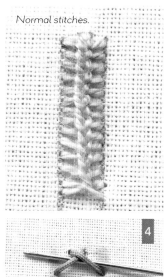

Normal stitches.

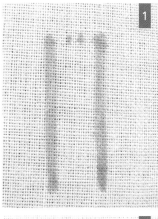

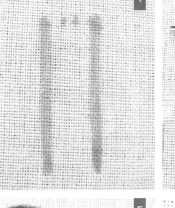

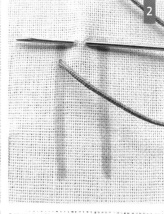

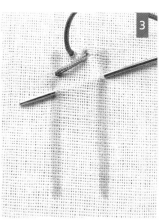

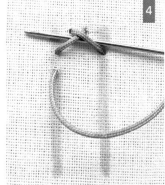

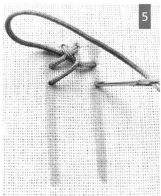

Finished enlarged and spaced stitches.

Begin by drawing two parallel lines and two dots (step 1). The step photographs show the stitches enlarged and spaced for clarity.

VERMICELLI STITCH

The green thread meanders around but should not cross over itself at any point.

WHIPPED BACKSTITCH

WHIPPED BLANKET STITCH

a.k.a. Whipped buttonhole stitch

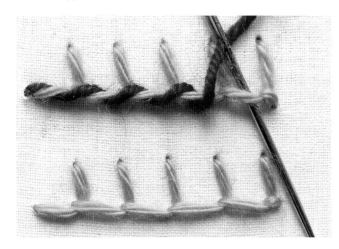

WHIPPED CHAIN STITCH

Chain stitch.

WHIPPED FLY STITCH

WHIPPED OPEN CHAIN STITCH

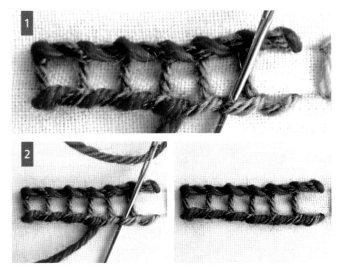

WHIPPED RUNNING STITCH

WHIPPED STEM STITCH

While whipping, go either in the same direction as the stitches, or the opposite. Use thread of the same or a contrasting colour.

WHIPPED STRAIGHT STITCH

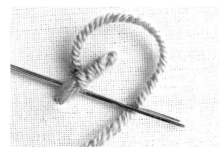

Threads of contrasting colours are shown here for clarity. Use the same colour thread for the Straight stitch and the wrapping.

WOVEN BAND

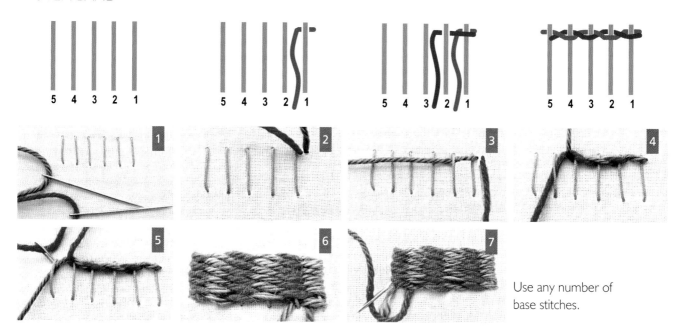

Use any number of base stitches.

WOVEN BAR

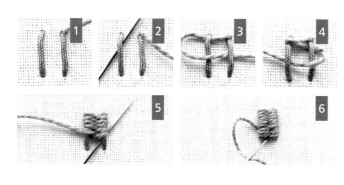

WOVEN FILLING (SOLID) 2 × 2

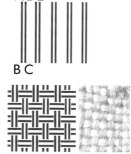

Step 1: To make warp threads, work stitches in pairs, leaving very little space between them.

Step 2: Weaving (weft threads). The weft stitches should also be in pairs (double-stitches), so work the weaving in two steps. First weave over and under the pairs of warp stitches, using one thread only. Now go the same way with a second thread. The first double-stitch is finished. Do the same for the second double stitch, going over where the first went under and vice versa.

WOVEN FILLING (SPACED BARS)

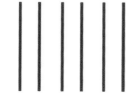
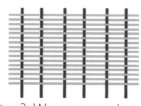

Step 1: Work spaced stitches for warp threads.

Step 2: Weave over and under these stitches (weft threads).

WOVEN WHEEL

Fairy designs

Jacobean crewel designs often remind me of fairy tales. This is what gave me the idea to dedicate this book to my favourite folk stories and fairy tales. These stories, which have been close to my heart since childhood, come from all over the world: the USA, Denmark, France, Russia and Poland. They all teach kindness, generosity, courage, faith and hope. The plot of one of these tales, *Cinderella*, can be found, with small variations, in the folklore of many different countries.

The variable nature of fairy tales has inspired me to try out variations in the stitching of these designs, and I encourage you to experiment for yourselves. Play with colour and texture, use different threads and stitches and replace anything or everything! I truly believe that this will do wonders for your stitching.

Colour

All of the smaller designs in this book derive from the largest one, the Tree of Happiness, and each one has its own dominant colour. When they are all brought together in the Tree of Happiness design (see detail opposite), they display all the colours of the rainbow.

RED: SCARLET SAILS 116

YELLOW/ORANGE: CREWEL WALTZ 128

GREEN: EMERALD CITY 94

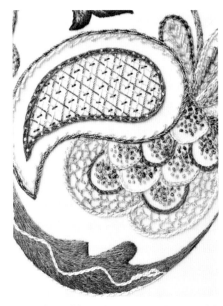

BLUE/INDIGO: THE BLUE BEAD 80

VIOLET: CREWEL WALTZ 128

How to start

See page 8 for the conversion chart from DMC thread to Appleton wool. Pages 10 to 15 show various options for stitching the same area. And do remember of course that it is not necessary to use all the stitches featured in the instructions for each design. Feel free to reduce their number for a totally new effect. Certainly the work order is never fixed.

To make a start, scan the design and trace it onto the fabric (see page 9). Fix the fabric into your favourite embroidery hoop or frame and enjoy stitching. Happy adventures in Crewel Land!

A detail from the Tree of Happiness deisgn.

Tree of Happiness

Each design in this book is dedicated to a particular fairy tale, except for the first and the last, which originate in my own life. Every now and then life supplies us with a story worthy of a good fairy tale. The story of the Tree of Happiness is a funny, strange and happy one. It is the story which inspired this book.

Once upon a time, in winter, I had a nasty case of the 'flu. What made things even worse was that the illness stopped me from sleeping. To cheer myself up I started reading. As it happened, I picked up *The Gulag Archipelago* by Alexandr Solzhenitsyn. The book describes the horrors of the gulags, the Soviet forced labour camps and the terrible life of the prisoners who suffered and died there. The author, a historian, became a gulag prisoner himself, and gave his own experience along with evidence from legal documents, reports, interviews and diaries. When my husband noticed me reading this book, he teased me: 'Are you are trying to make yourself feel better by reading about people having an even worse time than you?'

To take the wind out of his sails, I started drawing instead. Soon I had a whole bunch of sketches for new crewel designs, and I wanted to join them up into one huge project, which I needed for my crewel classes. We usually study dozens of stitches during a class, and you may know the feeling of itching to use them for a real pattern, not just for doodling.

The idea of a tree came into my head by chance. Long ago I stitched one for an embroidered towel to celebrate my wedding. This tree was in the style of Ukrainian folk embroidery of the Poltava region. Poltava is a big city in Ukraine with its own ancient stitching traditions, the Tree of Life pattern being one of them. The idea for this may have come from the Book of Genesis in tbe Bible. Of course, the Tree of Life is also one of the most popular designs in crewel embroidery. This is more likely to originate from printed patterns on fabric brought from India and Persia.

Whatever its origins, this design is popular in many different cultures, and is expressed not only in embroidery but also weaving, carpet making, pottery decoration and more.

Since I was going to make some changes to traditional crewel stitching and since I also badly needed a good portion of happiness at that time, I decided to make my tree idea into the Tree of Happiness design.

Enjoy planting it in your embroidery garden!

Size: 29.5 x 38.5cm
(11¾ x 15¼in)

Template: pages 151
This template is shown at half original size. Enlarge it to 200% before transferring it.

tip

You could also try working this design on a smaller scale, replacing some of stitches to fit the new size.

How to work the design

Have fun totally changing the colour scheme or just follow the one given in the instructions; replace Silk shading with any other stitch if you prefer, or take this chance to master it – whichever approach you choose, you will definitely have your own masterpiece at the end! Though the design looks rather complicated, its numerous elements provide dozens of options for stitching to suit any taste and embroidery habits.

WORK ORDER

Please note that the numbers on the stitching guides for the projects are just a key and do not imply an order of stitching. I would like to suggest three options. Since we usually judge ourselves by the skill level we have achieved in our stitching – and incidentally we are often our harshest critics in this regard – these approaches are based on the skill level you feel you have.

Advanced First have a look through the instructions, just for inspiration, then follow your own logic of stitching.

Intermediate Follow the Twelve zones order of stitching given in the instructions. Refer to the stitch guide on pages 22–47 where necessary.

Beginner Since you will probably be mastering embroidery techniques as you go, start with the simplest stitches and work stems and fine twigs all round the design first, then gradually come to the more intricate areas. This was the way I worked, for two reasons: to have a kind of warm-up and to get the impression of quick progress. Since the fine lines of the stems and twigs are scattered all around the area, you will soon get the satisfying feeling of finishing a good portion of the work and the rest of the job will not look so daunting. It's something about the psychology of stitching!

You will need

DMC PEARL COTTON THREAD SIZE 8:

SOLID COLOURS:

415 Pearl grey

640 Beige grey - vy dk

642 Beige grey - dk

738 Tan - vy lt

739 Tan - ultra vy lt

841 Beige brown - lt

842 Beige brown - vy lt

945 Tawny

Ecru

VARIEGATED:

51 Shades of orange

67 Shades of blue

69 Shades of cherry red

90 Shades of yellow

92 Shades of green

94 Shades of lt olive

99 Shades of burgundy

105 Shades of brown

125 Shades of seafoam green

DMC STRANDED COTTON THREAD:

SOLID COLOURS:

01 Grey - vy lt

163 Celadon green - med

164 Forest green - lt

225 Shell pink - ultra vy lt

351 Coral

352 Coral lt

353 Peach

368 Pistachio green - lt

501 Blue green - dk

502 Blue green

503 Blue green - med

517 Wedgwood - dk

518 Wedgwood - lt

519 Sky blue

522 Fern green

561 Jade - vy dk

647 Beaver grey - med

733 Olive green - med

741 Tangerine - med

742 Tangerine - lt

743 Yellow - med

744 Yellow - pale

745 Yellow - lt pale

815 Garnet - med

816 Garnet

830 Golden olive - dk

913 Nile green - med

987 Forest green - dk

988 Forest green - med

3022 Brown grey - med

3045 Yellow beige - dk

3078 Golden yellow - vy lt

3345 Hunter green - dk

3787 Brown grey -dk

3842 Wedwood - dk

Ecru

VARIEGATED:

4040 Shades of pale blue to pale green

4130 Shades of dk terracotta to copper

METALLIC:

E130 Dk burgundy, Sparkling green, Yellow and Dk blue

ATLAS POLYESTER THREAD

A Off-white

B Lt pink

C Dk pink

D Navy blue

E Dk navy blue

DMC SPECIAL DENTELLES:

Ecru

369 Pistachio green - vy dk

SEED BEADS:

15/o Miyuki Delica

Pale olive

15/o Toho Charlotte

One black bead for the bird's eye

key

Pearl cotton thread size 8 is marked P8 in the instructions, e.g. 415 Pearl grey is marked P8-415).
Variegated threads: now and then you will need to cut a section of a particular colour shade for stitching.

key

Stranded cotton thread is marked SC in the instructions, e.g. 01 Grey - vy lt is marked SC-01. The number in brackets means how many strands were used for the stitching e.g. SC-163(1) means one strand. For twisted cord always take one strand and then fold it in half. Optional: It is also possible to reduce the total number of colours by using only one shade of the following pairs to stitch both areas: 164 and 368; 561 and 163; 3078 and 745; 3022 and 647.

key

Atlas thread is marked At in the instructions, with letter for colour, e.g. Off-white Atlas thread is marked At-A. May be replaced with any kind of silk thread. This thread is about as fine as pearl cotton size 12.

key

Special dentelles thread is marked De in the instructions, e.g. Ecru, is marked De-Ecru. DMC Pearl cotton size 12 may be used instead.

The twelve zones

The whole design is divided into twelve zones or areas. Directions for stitching each zone are given as a separate image. Of course, there is no need to completely finish embroidering one zone before you start another. As for colours, kinds of threads and stitches, play around, alter whatever you would like, unleash your creativity. Sometimes we just need instructions to give us an idea of what to change.

1	BIRD
2	CROWNED FLOWER
3	POINTED LEAF, PEPPER AND TULIP
4	ROUND FRUIT
5	PUMPKIN
6	HEARTY FRUIT
7	SCALLOPED LEAF
8	TREE TRUNK
9	GREENERY
10	BUSH
11	DANCING FLOWER
12	FIRE-BUD

Free form zones

Now and then you will find stems which are not mentioned in the instructions at all. These are marked with red lines. This is sometimes because I am not convinced by the way I have stitched them. Sometimes, the particular method of stitching doesn't matter. In this case, either follow your own logic or use one of the following stitches to work these stems:

- Stem stitch, also possible in parallel rows
- Backstitch and/or Chain stitch, plain or whipped
- Raised chain stitch band
- Portuguese knotted stem stitch
- Tuning fork stitch

Use any green shade of stranded cotton or variegated pearl cotton in 92, 94 or 125 colour shades. You have plenty of these threads, so do not worry about running out of a colour.

The pink lines show stems without specific instructions.

Zone 1: Bird

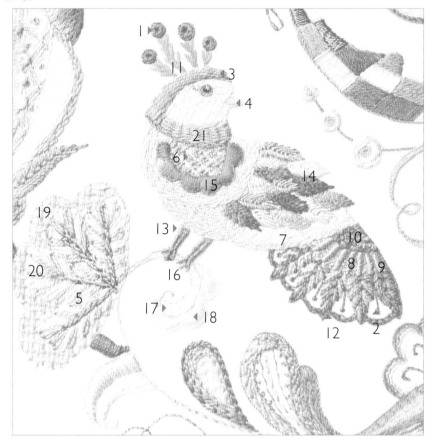

note

Please remember that the numbers allocated to each zone of the embroidery do not imply an order of stitching. The order in which you work is entirely up to you.

1. Buttonhole wheel SC-517 (1)
2. Pistil stitch SC-3345 (1)
3. Raised stem stitch P8-99
4. Satin stitch SC-726 (1)
5. Stem stitch At-D
6. Double lattice, 4-stitch couching SC-522 (1) + At-C
7. Bokhara couching P8-assorted (see opposite page), couched with SC-Ecru (1)

8. Ribbed filling stitch P8-642
9. Fly stitch leaf P8-69; 92
10. French knots P8-92, SC-3345; 816 (1)
11. Fly stitch P8-51
12. Heavy chain stitch SC-3345 (2)
13. Woven bar SC-936 (1)
14. Fly stitch leaf P8-99; At-B, C; see opposite page for details
15. Padded buttonhole scallops SC-4130 (1)

16. Lazy daisy stitch SC-936 (2)
17. Whipped open chain stitch SC-3022 (1)
18. Padded buttonhole stitch SC-225 (1)
19. Lattice + woven filling De-369; Ecru
20. Lazy daisy stitch P8-739, 841
21. Raised stem stitch SC-522 (2)
22. P8-945
23. P8-842

note

The number in brackets shows how many strands of stranded cotton thread were used.

tip

When working the eye of the bird, take one black size 15/o Toho Charlotte seed bead and attach it to the fabric sideways (as shown in the diagram). This will give the impression of a real eye with a highlight on its side.

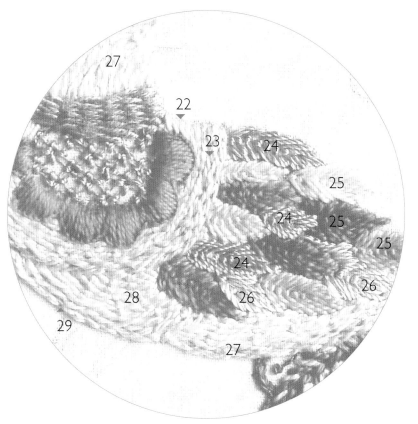

24. At-C
25. Sections of different shades of P8-99
26. At-B
27. P8-Ecru
28. P8-945
29. P8-738

Zone 2: Crowned flower

First stitch all the Silk shading areas, i.e. the heart inside the flower and the four green leaves on top. Embroider a line of Split stitch around each area before working Long and short stitches.

tip

This time work Split stitch using two strands of stranded cotton thread.

1. Fly stitch leaf SC-E130 metallic (1)

2. Whipped chain stitch SC-815 (2)

3. Tuning fork stitch P8-841

4. Stem stitch (to outline) P8-841

5. Fly stitch leaf + French knots P8-92

6. Chain stitch SC-815 (2)

7. Silk shading SC-815; 987; 163 (1)

8. Three overlapping rows of Herringbone stitch with French knots P8-841; 945

9. Raised stem stitch SC-Ecru (2)

10. Fly stitch leaf P8-945 (central leaf); P8-842 (two side leaves)

11. Lazy daisy stitch At-A

12. Raised stem stitch P8-99

13. Twisted cord SC-Ecru (1)

14. Padded buttonhole with bullion picots P8-90

15. Woven wheel P8-69

16. Silk shading + Lattice SC-815; 816; 351; 352; 353 (1); At-C

17. Lazy tuning fork stitch P8-94; 642

18. Buttonhole stitch P8-642

19. French knots P8-841

Zone 3: Pointed leaf, pepper and tulip

1. Backstitch P8-92
2. Chain stitch P8-125
3. Ribbed filling stitch P8-125; P8-94
4. Two Fly stitch leaves SC-3022 (2)
5. Raised fishbone stitch leaf SC-3345 (1)
6. Woven filling (solid) P8-92 lighter shades; SC-3022 (2)
7. Chain stitch SC-3842 (2)
8. Split stitch SC-988 (2) + Running stitch P8-92
9. Buttonhole stitch P8-92; 125
10. Silk shading SC-3842; 517; 519 (1)
11. Fly stitch leaf P8-67 whipped with SC-3842 (1)

12. Raised chain stitch band P8-92
13. Raised stem stitch P8-125
14. Whipped stem stitch P8-92
15. Raised fishbone stitch leaf SC-988 (1)
16. Silk shading P8-67; 125
17. Battlement couching P8-92
18. Overlapping buttonhole stitch P8-92
19. French knots SC-3842 (1)
20. Blanket stitch SC-3842 (1)
21. Woven filling (solid) P8-67

Zone 4: Round fruit

1. Lazy daisy stitch P8-739
2. Fly stitch P8-94
3. Lazy daisy stitch P8-841
4. Chain stitch P8-642
5. Twisted cord SC-502 (1)
6. Whipped backstitch SC-3345 (1)
7. Lattice At-A + Double lattice AT-E + Fly stitch couching At-D
8. Fly stitch (to fix lattice) At-D
9. Rope stitch SC-503 (2)
10. Chain stitch P8-125
11. Heavy chain SC-3345 (2)
12. Woven filling (solid) SC-4040 (2)
13. Whipped blanket stitch SC assorted; see diagram opposite
14. French knot SC assorted (1); see diagram opposite
15. Woven filling (spaced bars) SC-517; 518; 519 (2)
16. Chain stitch SC-3842 (2)
17. Satin stitch blocks: assorted SC (1) and At; see diagram opposite

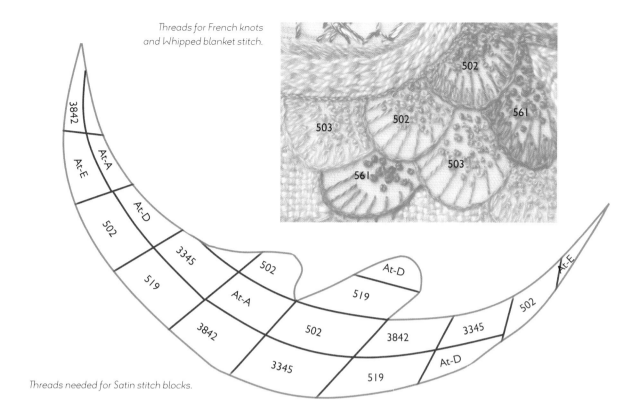

*Threads for French knots
and Whipped blanket stitch.*

Threads needed for Satin stitch blocks.

Zone 5: Pumpkin

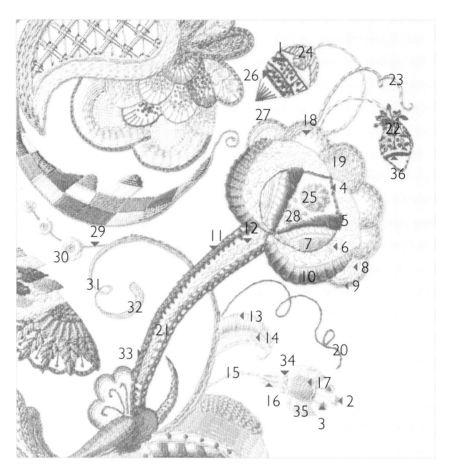

1. French knot + Pistil stitch SC-815 (1)

2. Rhodes stitch SC-4040 (1)

3. French knot. Centre: SC-517 (2); knots around it: SC-503 (1)

4. Split stitch SC-815; 3345 (2)

5. Rope stitch SC-3345 (2)

6. Fly stitch SC-225; 3078; 742 (1)

7. Raised stem stitch P8-738

8. French knots SC-Ecru (1)

9. Chain stitch P8-841

10. Ribbed filling stitch P8-69

11. Twisted cord SC-3345 (1)

12. Raised chain stitch band P8-92

13. Padded buttonhole stitch P8-945 + Straight stitch placed in between P8-738

14. Raised stem stitch SC-4040 (1)

15. Double-threaded backstitch P8-125 threaded with SC-503 (1)

16. Ribbed filling stitch P8-125

17. Padded buttonhole stitch P8-67

18. Blanket stitch P8-738

19. French knots SC-3078 (1); Ecru (2)

20. Twisted cord SC-3345 (1)

21. Tuning fork stitch P8-92

22. Pistil stitch SC-815 (1)

23. Double threaded backstitch P8-92; SC-733 (1)

24. Fly stitch leaf SC-3345 (1); 164 (2)

25. Ribbed spider web P8-90 + French knots between the ribs SC-742 (2)

26. Herringbone stitch + Chain stitch SC-815 (2)

27. Straight stitch SC-815 (1)

28. French knots SC-3078 (1); SC-742 (2)

29. Whipped stem stitch SC-3022 (1)

30. Stem stitch roses: French knot centres SC-741 (3); Stem stitch petals SC-225 (6)

31. Stem stitch SC-647 (1)

32. Loop stitch + Twisted cord SC-647 (1)

33. Raised chain stitch band P8-94

34. Raised chain stitch band P8-125

35. Raised stem stitch P8-67

36. Chain stitch SC-815 (2)

note

Perhaps you can think of your own way of stitching the two fruit capsules that appear above the pumpkin. If so, do not hesitate to use it.

Zone 6: Hearty fruit

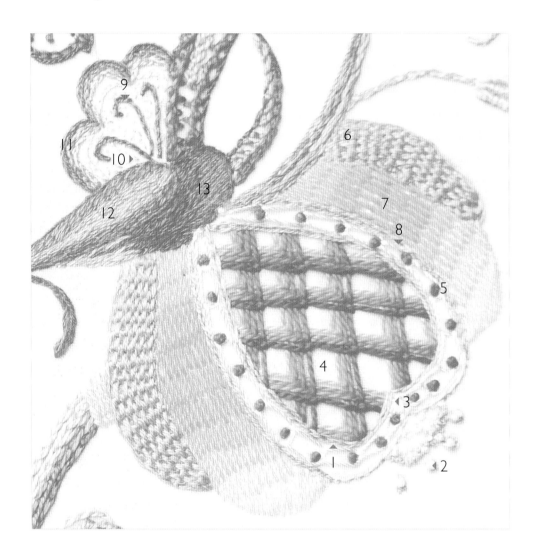

1. Whipped chain stitch SC-647 (1)
2. French knot SC-3078; 647 (1); At-A
3. Wide chain stitch At-A
4. Battlement couching P8-69
5. French knot SC-815 (1)
6. Raised chain stitch band SC-733 (2)
7. Burden stitch worked in twisted cord SC-741 through 745 (1)

8. Chain stitch SC-647 (1)
9. Split stitch SC-3842 (2)
10. Seeding stitches SC-519; 4040 (1)
11. Chain stitch SC-3842; 517 (1)
12. Raised stem stitch SC-733; 830 (1)
13. Silk shading SC-3345 (1)

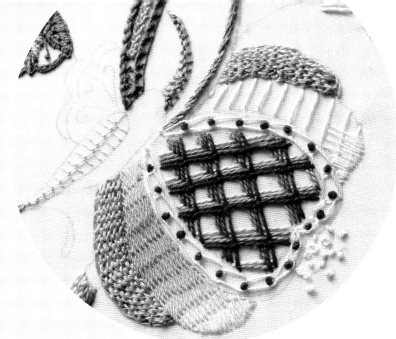

Part way through stitching.

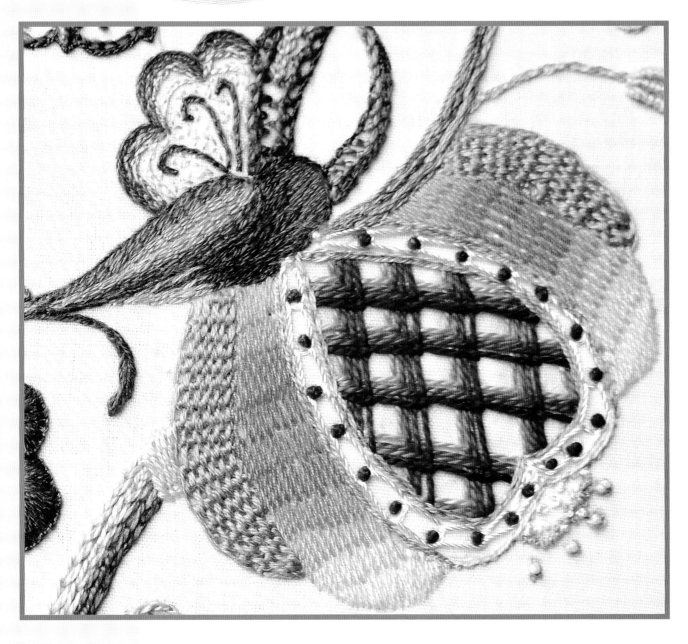

Zone 7: Scalloped leaf

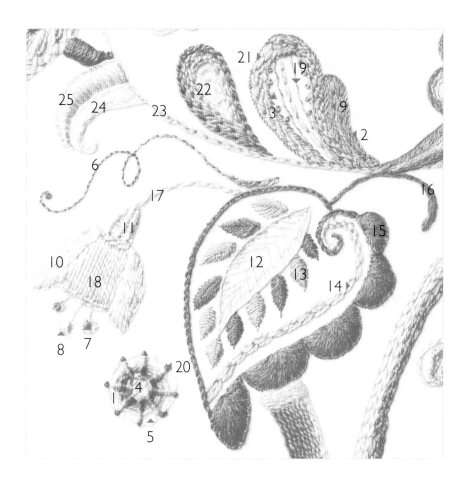

1. Ribbed spider web SC-502; 503 (1)
2. Twisted cord SC-502 (1)
3. French knot SC-502 (1)
4. Woven wheel SC-501 (1)
5. Chain stitch SC-225 (2)
6. Backstitch SC-3345 (1)
7. French knot: Centre: SC-517 (2); Around the centre: SC-503 (1)
8. Rhodes stitch SC-4040 (1)
9. Raised stem stitch SC-830 (1)
10. Raised stem stitch P8-67
11. Ribbed filling stitch P8-125
12. Open fishbone stitch + Straight stitch in between SC-503 (1)
13. Raised fishbone stitch leaf SC-988; 3345 (1)
14. Tuning fork stitch P8-125
15. Padded buttonhole scallops SC-3345 (1)
16. Rope stitch SC-3345 (2)
17. Backstitch P8-125
18. Padded buttonhole stitch P8-67
19. Whipped running stitch SC-502 (1)
20. French knot SC-501 (2)
21. Tuning fork stitch P8-125
22. Chain stitch P8-94
23. Chain stitch SC-647 (1)
24. Raised stem stitch SC-4040 (1)
25. Padded buttonhole stitch P8-945 + Straight stitch in between P8-738

Part way through stitching.

Zone 8: Tree trunk

1. Raised stem stitch SC-743 (2)
2. Chain stitch P8-945
3. Chain stitch P8-105
4. Portuguese knotted stem stitch P8-642
5. Twisted cord SC-3022 (1)
6. Whipped running stitch SC-3022 (1)
7. Backstitch P8-92
8. Straight stitch SC-517 (1)
9. Raised stem stitch P8-105
10. Chain stitch P8-105
11. Portuguese knotted stem stitch P8-92
12. Chain stitch P8-642

Zone 9: Greenery

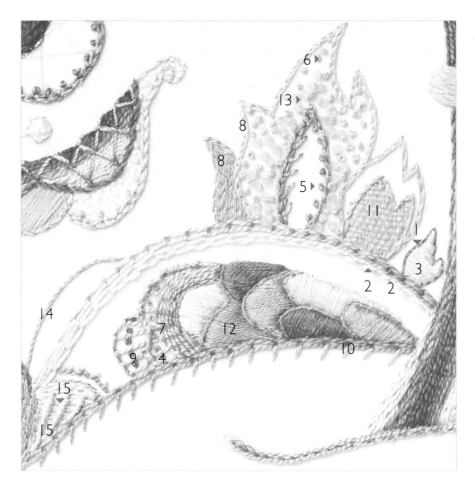

1. Backstitch SC-988 (1)
2. Chain stitch P8-92
3. Satin stitch P8-92
4. French knot SC-988 (2)
5. Chain stitch with French knots SC-3022 (2)
6. French knots SC-164 (2)
7. Raised stem stitch P8-642
8. Chain stitch SC-733 (2); SC-164 (2)
9. French knot SC-3345 (2)
10. Mountmellick stitch P8-92
11. Woven filling (solid) SC-733 (2); 647 (2)
12. Padded satin stitch: Assorted SC (1); see diagram below
13. Seed beads
14. Twisted cord SC-988 (1)
15. Ribbed filling stitch SC-01 (2)

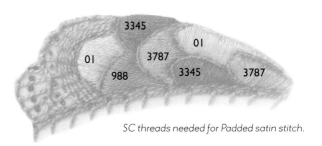

SC threads needed for Padded satin stitch.

Zone 10: Bush

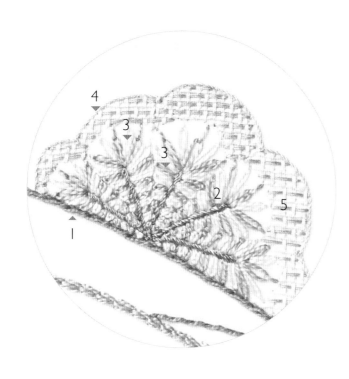

1. Rope stitch P8-92
2. Stem stitch At-D
3. Lazy daisy stitch P8-739; 841
4. Twisted cord SC-647 (1)
5. Lattice stitch + woven filling De-369; Ecru

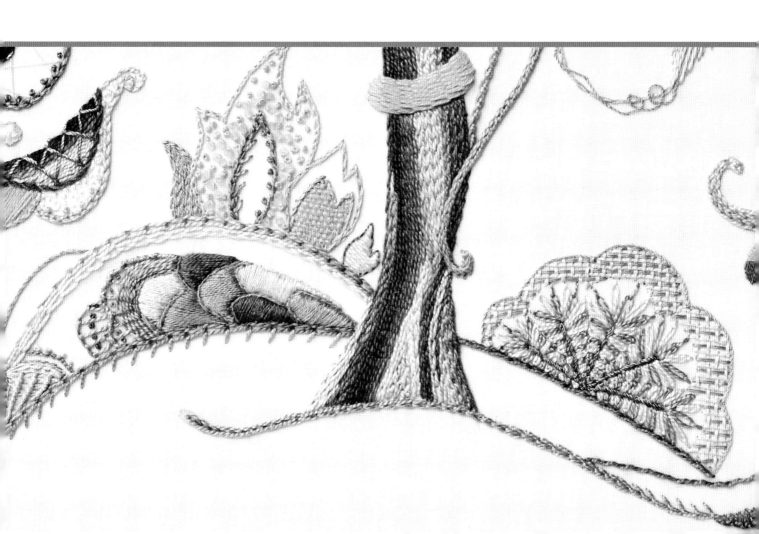

Zone 11: Dancing flower

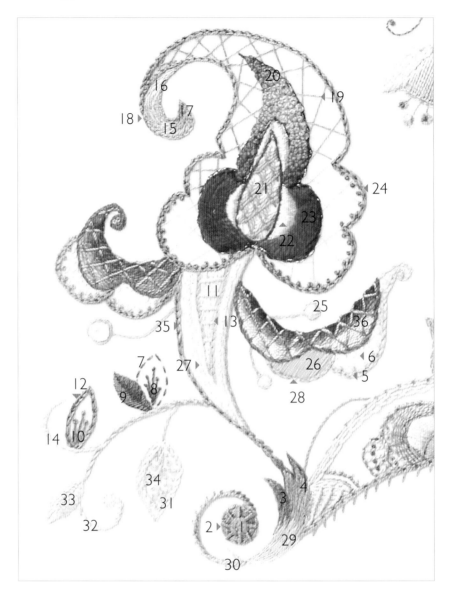

1. Woven wheel SC-3787 (2)	13. Chain stitch SC-913 (2)	25. Rhodes stitch SC-3078 (1)
2. Ribbed spider web SC-936 (2)	14. Stem stitch P8-92	26. Satin stitch SC-913 (2)
3. Silk shading SC-3789 (1)	15. Silk shading SC-647 (1)	27. Chain stitch At-A
4. Silk shading SC-3022 (1)	16. Silk shading SC-01 (1)	28. Split stitch SC-913 (2)
5. Chain stitch P8-125	17. Silk shading SC-3022 (1)	29. Silk shading SC-647 (1)
6. Seeding stitch At-A	18. Stem stitch SC-3022 (2)	30. Twisted chain stitch P8-92
7. Running stitch SC-3345 (2)	19. Herringbone stitch SC-3022 (1)	31. Chain stitch P8-92
8. Pistil stitch SC-3345 (2)	20. French knots P8-69	32. Portuguese knotted stem stitch P8-92
9. Raised fishbone stitch leaf SC-3345 (2)	21. Battlement couching P8-90	33. Fly stitch leaf P8-92
10. Pistil stitch SC-988 (2)	22. Padded satin stitch SC-225 (1)	34. Seed beads + French knot SC-647 (2)
11. Ribbed filling stitch SC-3078 (2)	23. Raised stem stitch P8-90	35. Chain stitch SC-936 (2)
12. Chain stitch SC-988 (2)	24. French knots SC-936 (1)	36. Raised stem stitch P8-99 + Lattice At-C

Zone 12: Fire-bud

1. Twisted cord SC-3787 (1)

2. Raised fishbone stitch leaf SC-647; 3345 (1)

3. Silk shading SC-936 (1)

4. Silk shading SC-647 (1)

5. Silk shading SC-3022 (1)

6. Silk shading SC-3787 (1)

7. Silk shading SC-647 (1)

8. Silk shading SC-3022 (1)

9. Silk shading SC-3787 (1)

10. Padded buttonhole stitch SC-368 (2)

11. Chain stitch P8-94

12. Chain stitch P8-125

13. Battlement couching P8-125

14. Satin stitch blocks: Assorted SC (1); see diagram opposite

15. Raised stem stitch P8-99; 945 + Lattice At-B

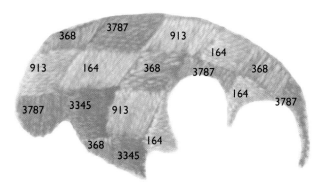

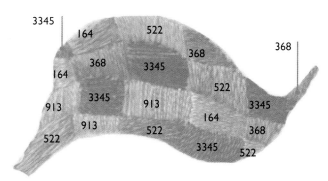

SC threads for satin stitch blocks.

THE FIRE-BUD'S CHECKED LEAVES

This shows the layout for the thread colours that I used, but I suggest picking up a selection of at least five shades of green, then scattering them over the area at random. To do this, the work order is as follows. Using a fabric marker or HB pencil, divide each leaf into zones for Satin stitch blocks. I prefer not to make them square or rectangular (as in the diagram with black lines, right) but to follow the outlines of each leaf (see the diagram with pink lines). Mark the placement of Satin stitches within each particular block (see the orange lines). Now pick up thread of any colour from your selection and work Satin stitch within any three blocks of the area. Of course those blocks are supposed to be scattered around, not just the neighbouring ones. Keep to the marked direction of Satin stitches. Do the same with each of the threads, varying the number of blocks for any particular colour until all the area is stitched.

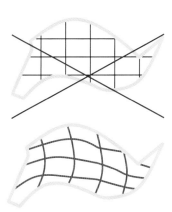

The wrong (top) and right ways to mark out the Satin stitch blocks.

The orange lines show the alternating directions of the Satin stitching.

Size: 24.8 x 15.8cm
(9¾ x 6½in)

Template: page 152

The Blue Bead

The first magical story I remember from early childhood is *The Blue Bead* by Polish writer Maria Krüger. Written in 1959, this novel for children is still required reading for 7 to 9-year-old pupils in Poland. A little girl called Karolcia accidently finds a small blue bead in a crack in the floor of her old home while her family is moving into a new apartment. The bead turns out to be magical and this is the start of Karolcia's adventures. She begins to discover the wonderful properties of the blue bead soon after arriving in her new home. She decides to clean the dust off it and rubs it with soap. Then she notices, much to her astonishment, that a pea-sized object has started growing from it, and this finally turns into a soap bubble-sized ball. This magic bubble speaks to Karolcia and they become friends. Together they conquer an evil witch and find out what true friendship is. The big round element in the middle of this design makes me think of Karolcia's blue bead, and that is how the design got its name.

My Brussels stitch story

I have a personal story about Brussels stitch, which is used in this design. I was thirteen when I first found it in an embroidery book under the name 'Artistic darning'. This intrigued me and I decided to try it that very evening. As luck would have it, my younger brother came home from football with a hole in his trousers. Since our Mum had given me the duty of mending his clothes, I got to work at once, with rare enthusiasm and the promise of decorating his trousers.

In the end I was deeply disappointed with the new stitch and had to do the job again with the usual darning technique. Worse, I concluded that this beautiful stitch was useless and I didn't try it again until, as an adult, I saw its real beauty in needlelace. There was nothing wrong with it at all, but the name had confused me into using it for the wrong purpose! And now I could guess why it had been called Artistic darning: the book in which I found it was published in the former Soviet Union, where everything had to have a utilitarian purpose, as though to convince people that art is not important in our lives. A sad and silly fact about the reality of those times – but at least it gave me a funny story.

The five zones

The five stitching zones for this design appear in the instructions as they are marked in the diagram.

1 THE BEAD

2 BOTTOM LEFT LEAF

3 TOP RIGHT LEAF

4 TOP LEFT CLUSTER

5 BOTTOM RIGHT CLUSTER

Some of the six smallest elements of this design vary in stitching, for example they might use the same technique but have different colours of thread. If you really like a particular way of stitching these areas, just repeat it for all six elements.

You will need

DMC PEARL COTTON THREAD SIZE 8:

VARIEGATED:

67 Shades of blue

94 Shades of lt olive

DMC STRANDED COTTON THREAD:

SOLID COLOURS:

311 Navy blue – med

518 Wedgwood – lt

519 Sky blue

828 Blue – ultra vy lt

3756 Baby blue – ultra vy lt

3760 (806) Wedgwood – med

3765 Peacock blue – vy dk

3865 Winter white

ATLAS POLYESTER THREAD:

At-A Off-white

At-B Blue

At-C Dark blue

key

Pearl cotton thread size 8 is marked P8 in the instructions, e.g. 415 Pearl grey is marked P8–415.

Stranded cotton thread is marked SC in the instructions, e.g. 519 Sky blue is marked SC–519.

The number in brackets means how many strands were used for the stitching e.g. SC–311 (1) means one strand.

For twisted cord always take one strand and then fold it in half.

Atlas thread is marked At in the instructions, with letter for colour, e.g. Off-white is At-A. May be replaced with any kind of silk thread. It is about as fine as pearl cotton size 12.

Zone 1: The bead

1. Scroll stitch P8-94
2. Hungarian braided chain stitch SC-3765 (2)
3. French knots SC-3865 (1)
4. Lattice stitch + woven filling At-A; B; C
5. Portuguese border stitch P8-94
6. Chain stitch P8-94
7. French knots At-C; SC-3765 (1)

8. Chain stitch Assorted: SC-518; 828; 3765 (2)
9. Twisted single Brussels stitch SC-518; 3760 (2)
10. Silk shading SC-518; 3760; 3765 (1)
11. Twisted cord At-A
12. Split stitch P8-94
13. Twisted chain stitch P8-94
14. Chain stitch At-B

note

Please remember that the numbers allocated to each zone of the embroidery do not imply an order of stitching. The order in which you work is entirely up to you.

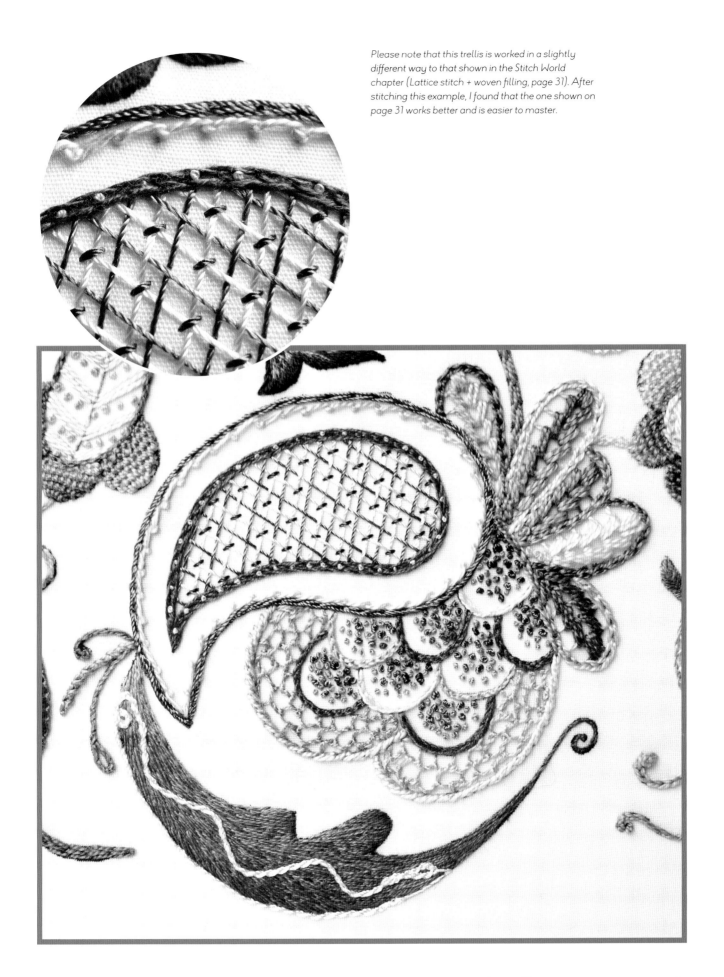

Please note that this trellis is worked in a slightly different way to that shown in the Stitch World chapter (Lattice stitch + woven filling, page 31). After stitching this example, I found that the one shown on page 31 works better and is easier to master.

Zone 2: Bottom left leaf

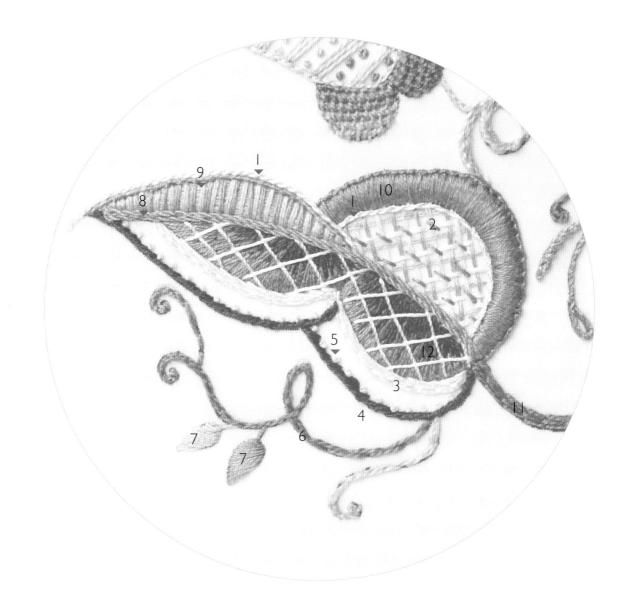

1. Twisted cord At-A
2. Lattice + woven filing SC-828; 3760; 3765 (2)
3. Rope stitch + Chain stitch SC-3865 (2)
4. Rope stitch SC-311 (2)
5. French knot SC-3865 (1)
6. Split stitch P8-94

7. Satin stitch SC-519; 3760 (1)
8. Twisted cord SC-3765 (1)
9. Buttonhole stitch SC-518; 3760 (2)
10. Padded buttonhole stitch SC-3765 (2)
11. Tuning fork stitch P8-94
12. Silk shading SC-311; 3760; 3765 (1)

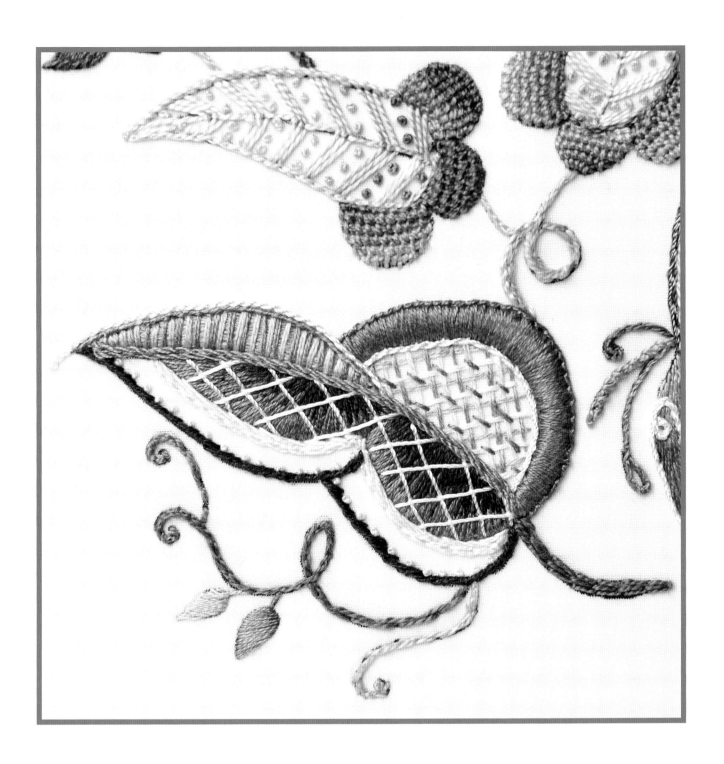

Zone 3: Top right leaf

1. Twisted cord SC-311; 3760 (1)

2. French knot SC-3756; 311 (1)

3. Rope stitch SC-828 (2)

4. Chain stitch SC-3865 (2)

5. Padded buttonhole stitch SC-311; 3765 (2); At-A

6. Chain stitch SC-3756 (2)

7. Lattice + woven filling SC-828; 3765 (2)

8. Rope stitch SC-3865; 828 (2)

9. French knot SC-3765 (2)

10. Woven band SC-376; 518 (2)

11. Silk shading SC-828; 3760 (1) + Lattice At-C; couched with SC-3765 (1)

12. Padded buttonhole stitch SC-311; 3765 (2)

13. Stem stitch P8-94

14. Satin stitch SC-518; 3760 (1)

15. Heavy chain stitch P8-94

16. Twisted chain stitch P8-94

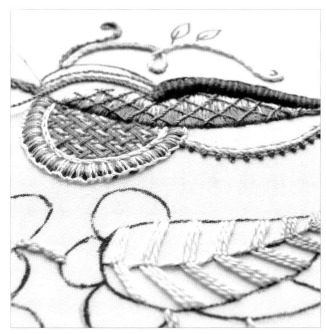

Part way through stitching.

Zone 4: Top left cluster

1. French knot SC-3765 (1)
2. Satin stitch SC-311 (2)
3. Chain stitch SC-3765 (1)
4. Silk shading SC-519 (2) + Lattice SC-311 (1)
5. Satin stitch SC-828; 3765 (2)
6. Satin stitch SC-311 (2) + Feather stitch SC-3765 (1)
7. Feather stitch P8-67
8. French knot P8-94
9. Stem stitch and/or Split stitch P8-94
10. Split stitch P8-94

11. Corded single Brussels stitch P8-94
12. Buttonhole stitch SC-311; 3765 (2)
13. Tuning fork stitch P8-94
14. French knot SC-3765 (1)
15. Backstitch P8-94
16. Chain stitch P8-94
17. Whipped wheel P8-67
18. Silk shading SC-828; 3760 (2) + Feather stitch SC-311; 518 (1)
19. Bullion knot P8-94

Part way through stitching.

Zone 5: Bottom right cluster

1. Bullion knot P8-94
2. Fly stitch leaf SC-3765 (2)
3. Silk shading SC-519 (2) + Lattice SC-828 (1)
4. Chain stitch P8-94
5. Portuguese knotted stem stitch P8-94
6. Split stitch P8-94

7. Whipped wheel P8-67
8. Chain stitch P8-94
9. Satin stitch SC-518; 3765 (1)
10. Split stitch P8-94
11. Silk shading SC-519; 828 (1)

Part way through stitching.

Emerald City

The Emerald City is the capital of the Land of Oz in Lyman Frank Baum's Oz books. *The Wonderful Wizard of Oz* and its sequels were my favourites at school. To add to the joy of reading all these books, they were given to me as a birthday present from my godfather whom I loved dearly. At that time I was in a folk dance group for schoolchildren, and we were invited to take part in huge concerts during our winter holidays. This was more than we had ever dreamed of, and though we had to spend the whole school holiday performing morning till night, we were in seventh heaven! The organizers even gave us a present each, and that is how I got my first camera. Such sweet memories and all connected in my mind to the Oz books, which I read during the short breaks between performances.

In the books, Dorothy and her friends longed to get to the Emerald City in the hope that its ruler would grant them their wishes. Walking along the yellow brick road in the Land of Oz, they saw the city and its shining towers from afar.

The green top of the flower in this design and the shining gold thread and gold-plated seed beads remind me of this moment in their adventure. Besides, everything was emerald green in the Emerald City because of the coloured sunglasses all the citizens and visitors wore – and this is also the dominant colour of this embroidery.

Dorothy's kind heart, Scarecrow's devoted heart, the Iron Woodcutter's loving heart and the Cowardly Lion's brave heart helped the friends get what each of them was seeking. The heart is the central element of this design, portrayed in pink and burgundy shades.

Some of the stitches are very simple, others are a bit more intricate, and there are also some rather tricky ones. The highlight of the latter group is Pleated braid stitch. Look through the instructions first and then have a try on a doodle cloth before using it for the design itself. I think this is the stitch to blow the illusion that embroidery is easy! I've had great fun, however, proving that it is worth the effort!

The other techniques are much easier, and I'm willing to bet that Granitos, Bayeux stitch, Rope stitch and Tuning fork stitch will become your favourites forever.

Size: 12.6 x 14cm
(5 x 5½in)

Template: page 153

You will need

DMC PEARL COTTON THREAD SIZE 8:

SOLID COLOURS:

945 Tawny

959 Sea green med

VARIEGATED:

94 Shades of lt olive

99 Shades of burgundy

111 Brown to bright yellow

125 Shades of seafoam green

DMC STRANDED COTTON THREAD:

SOLID COLOURS:

B5200 Bright white

3348 Yellow green lt

3822 Straw – lt

VARIEGATED:

4040 Shades of pale blue to pale green

METALLIC:

Gold thread (any brand)

SEED BEADS:

15/0 Toho gold rocailles permanent finish galvanized starlight

15/0 Miyuki Delica, white

key

Pearl cotton thread size 8 is marked P8 in the instructions, e.g. 945 Tawny is marked P8–945.

Stranded cotton thread is marked SC in the instructions, e.g. B5200 Bright white is marked SC–B5200.

The number in brackets means how many strands were used for the stitching, e.g. SC–163(1) means one strand.

For twisted cord always take one strand and then fold it in half.

Zone 1: The central element

The central element of the design is divided in the instructions into three parts: the top, the middle and the bottom. It might help to start with the middle, then do the top and the bottom after that.

French knots Among all the crewel designs in this book, this one is a champion for the number of French knots used! The knots really deserve their prominence, however. Notice how the textured area at the bottom is knotted all over, creating quite a different effect from its surroundings, even though the thread colour is almost the same. The right and left sepals also show knots in flowing shades of green, as well as two contrasting greens scattered at random around the top parts. Another great technique of crewel stitching that has come down to us through the centuries is to place French knots at equal intervals along a row of any outline stitch, e.g. Rope stitch in this design. When they are combined, they remind me of the decoration on top of Gothic cathedrals.

Needlelace Twisted single Brussels stitch (a.k.a. Twisted detached buttonhole) fills in the heart shape in the centre. Its rows are placed horizontally, but they can go in any direction you like. Again, using variegated thread adds interest to the stitching.

Gold seed beads Outline the sepals in olive thread first, then attach the beads and finish by scattering French knots around the area.

Burden stitch Here this is worked on top of one-colour Silk shading, and the couching stitches are spaced (see Burden stitch 2, page 24).

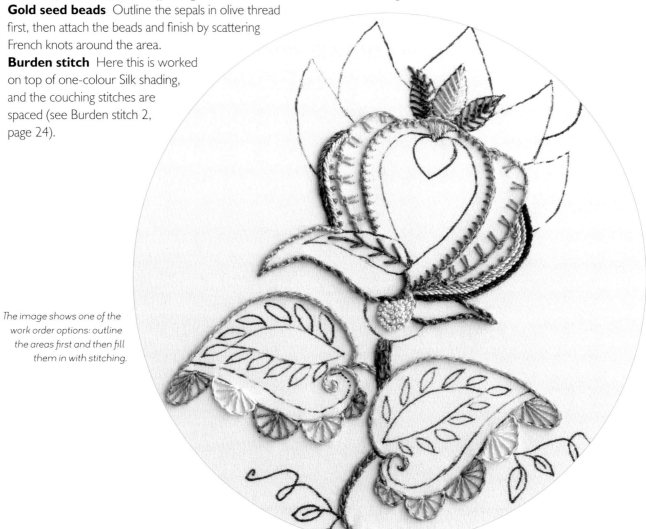

The image shows one of the work order options: outline the areas first and then fill them in with stitching.

MIDDLE

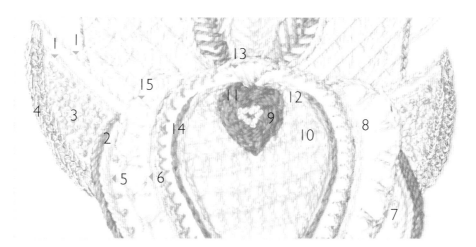

note

Please remember that the numbers allocated to each zone of the embroidery do not imply an order of stitching. The order in which you work is entirely up to you.

1. Chain stitch SC-3822 (2)

2. Rope stitch P8-99

3. French knot P8-125; SC-3348 (1)

4. Plaited braid stitch Gold thread

5. French knot P8-99

6. Couching SC-3822 (6 threads couched with 1)

7. Seed beads Miyuki delica 15/0

8. French knot SC-B5200 (1)

9. French knot SC-3822 (1)

10. Twisted single Brussels stitch P8-99

11. Woven wheel P8-99

12. Split stitch P8-99

13. Buttonhole stitch P8-125 + Straight stitch SC-3348 (2) in the gaps

14. Palestrina stitch P8-94

15. German knotted buttonhole stitch P8-125

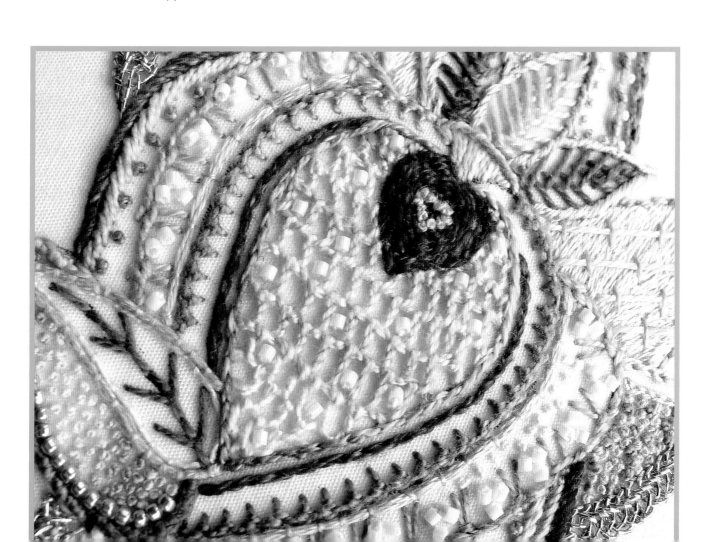

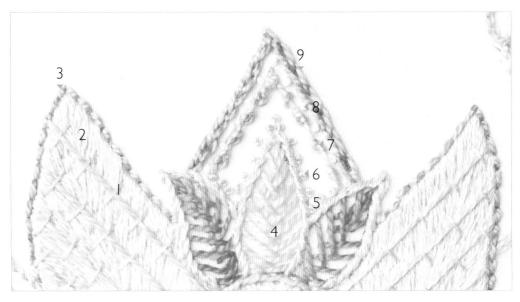

1. Burden stitch 2 P8-125
2. Silk shading SC-3348 (1)
3. Backstitch P8-125

4. Open fishbone stitch P8-111
5. Rope stitch SC-3822 (2)
6. French knot SC-3822 (1)

7. Coral stitch P8-125
8. French knot SC-D5200 (1)
9. Chain stitch P8-125

BOTTOM

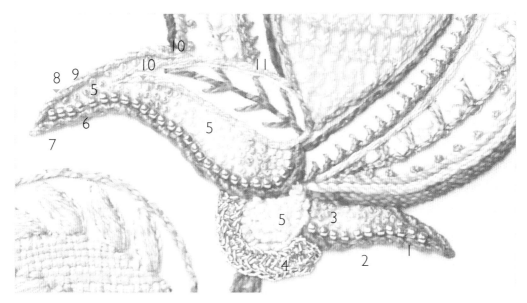

1. Couching (seed beads: Toho 15/0)

2. Portuguese knotted stem stitch P8-94

3. French knot P8-125

4. Plaited braid stitch Gold thread

5. French knot P8-125

6. Couching, seed beads, Toho 15/0

7. Portuguese knotted stem stitch P8-94

8. Portuguese knotted stem stitch P8-94

9. French knot P8-125

10. Couching SC-3822 (6 threads couched with 1 thread)

11. Fern stitch P8-94

Zone 2: Leaves and tendrils

Work the other leaf in a similar way to the one shown here.

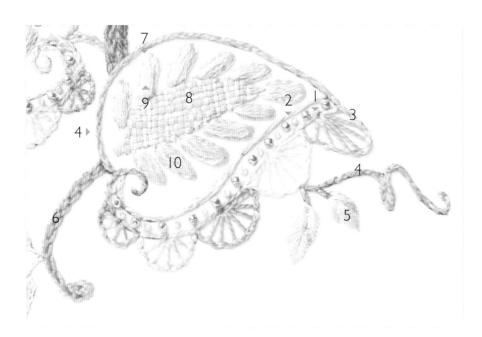

1. French knot P8-125
2. Stem stitch P8-959
3. Buttonhole scallops P8-125
4. Split stitch P8-125
5. Raised fishbone stitch leaf SC-4040 (1)

6. Tuning fork stitch P8-111
7. Chain stitch SC-3348 (1)
8. Woven filling 2 x 2 P8-945; 959
9. Granitos SC-3348 (2) outlined with chain stitch SC-3348 (1)
10. Granitos SC-3822 (2) outlined with chain stitch SC-3822 (1)

Elisa

Size: 27.3 x 12.4cm
(10¾ x 5in)

Template: page 154

This design is named after the heroine of *The Wild Swans*, a fairytale by Hans Christian Andersen. Elisa was a 15-year-old princess who rescued her eleven brothers after an evil queen cast a spell that turned them into swans. To do this, Elisa had to gather nettles and knit them into shirts, taking a vow of silence during all her work, because speaking a word would kill her brothers. She suffered a lot, not only from the pain of the nettles' stings, but also from people accusing her of witchcraft. She was sentenced to death, yet kept knitting, determined to finish as much of her work as possible. In the end, all went well, although Elisa's youngest brother had a wing instead of a hand for a little longer, because she did not manage to finish knitting one of the sleeves for his shirt in time.

A small difference in the colour shades of the tendrils in the very centre of the design reminds me of that wing, which finally turned back into a hand when Elisa got married. Also, the symmetrical parts of this design are worked from the same pattern repeated twice, which is reminiscent of a swan's wings and provides an opportunity to practise all the stitches twice. The pale pastel tones symbolize the touching tenderness of true love, devotion and self-sacrifice depicted in *The Wild Swans*.

One more distinctive feature of this design is that no Silk shading was used for its stitching. This is a bonus for those of us who have trouble with the shading technique or just dislike working it! Moreover, pearl cotton thread sizes 8 and 12 dominate in this design, and these are thicker than stranded cotton and so far easier to thread. This makes stitching quicker without compromising the beauty of the finished piece.

The twenty-nine varied stitches used for this design show the full range and richness of modern crewel embroidery. You might like to remember them and use them for future projects. Pay special attention to Fancy filling stitch: it is an easy yet rather unusual technique which helps to cover large areas in almost no time.

You will need

DMC PEARL COTTON THREAD SIZE 8:

SOLID COLOURS:

315 Antique mauve - med dk

320 Pistachio green - med

640 Beige grey – vy dk

760 Salmon

794 Cornflower blue – lt

841 Beige brown - lt

959 Sea green – med

3753 Antique blue – ultra vy lt

VARIEGATED:

99 Shades of burgundy

DMC PEARL COTTON THREAD SIZE 12:

SOLID COLOURS:

B5200 White

Blanc

503 Blue green - med

778 Antique mauve - vy lt

822 Beige grey - lt

842 Beige brown - vy lt

931 Antique blue – med

ATLAS POLYESTER THREAD:

A Bright white (as fine as Pearl Cotton size 12)

MIYUKI SEED BEADS:

15/0 DBS-374

15/0 DBS Old gold

15/0 Round, reddish orange from any manufacturer; even irregular shapes will do

key

Pearl cotton thread size 8 is marked P8 in the instructions, e.g. 320 Pistachio green is marked P8–320.

Pearl cotton thread size 12 is marked P12 in the instructions e.g. P12–503.

key

Atlas thread is marked At–A in the instructions.

Symmetrical parts

This design consists of two symmetrical parts which remind me of the spreading wings of a swan (though in the design they have rotational rather than mirror symmetry). Whenever I work on designs with symmetrical parts or repeated elements, I prefer to stitch all the similar areas over the whole piece before continuing with the rest. This is for two reasons: firstly it makes it more likely that the repeated parts will come out looking the same. Secondly, if you work in this way, you won't get too bored of repeatedly working the same stitch. This is because you will be stitching it in a row: a little trick that makes it feel as though you're stitching one bigger area rather than two or three repeated zones. At least this is how it works for me and – who knows – it might be helpful for you as well.

The four zones

1 THE CENTRAL PART   **2 FLOWER**   **3 BLUEBELL AND LEAF**   **4 TEXTURED BLUEBELLS**

Zone 1: The central part

note

Please remember that the numbers allocated to each zone of the embroidery do not imply an order of stitching. The order in which you work is entirely up to you.

1. Couching (seed beads)
2. French knot P12-503
3. Split stitch P8-3753
4. Raised fishbone stitch leaf P12-822; 842
5. Pistil stitch P12-503 to couch the intersections of the lattice
6. Lattice P12-931

7. Rope stitch P8-760
8. Couching (thread) P12-842
9. Couching (seed beads)
10. Whipped open chain stitch P8-320
11. Portuguese knotted stem stitch P8-640

Left: part way through stitching

Below: finished.

Zone 2: Flower

1. Burden stitch 2 P12-503, worked over no other stitch
2. Couching (seed beads)
3. Double Brussels stitch P12-778
4. Scalloped buttonhole chain stitch P12-778, P8-640
5. Rope stitch P8-640
6. Satin stitch P12-503
7. Burden stitch 2 P12-842, over satin stitch
8. Double Brussels stitch P12-842
9. Rope stitch P8-841 or P12-842
10. Double Brussels stitch P12-842
11. Backstitch P8-841

12. Buttonhole wheel P8-99; 640
13. Fancy filling stitch – First striped layer: P8-640; 841
    Second layer: P12-Blanc
    Third layer: P12-931
14. Stem stitch P8-640
15. Double Brussels stitch P12-778
16. Double Brussels stitch P12-503
17. Ribbed filling stitch At-A
18. Double Brussels stitch P12-778
19. French knot P8-760 + Straight stitch P12-822
20. Bayeux stitch P12-B5200

Part way through stitching.

Zone 3: Bluebell and leaf

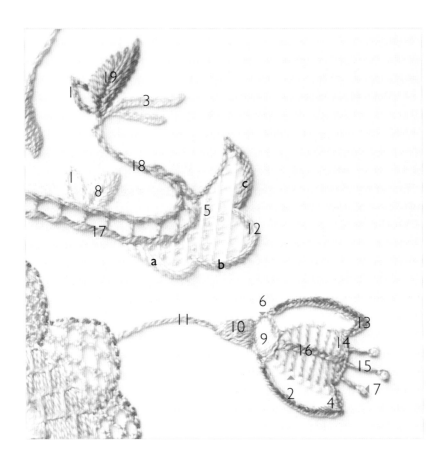

1. Split stitch P8-3753; 640
2. French knot P12-B5200
3. Heavy chain stitch P8-3753
4. Fly stitch At-A
5. French knot P12-822
6. Whipped backstitch P12-503
7. French knot P8-3753
8. Raised fishbone stitch leaf P8-3753
9. Satin stitch At-A
10. Raised stem stitch P12-503

11. Rope stitch P12-503
12. Rope stitch a P8-3753; b P8-794; c P12-931
13. Heavy chain stitch P12-931
14. Whipped backstitch P12-931
15. Whipped straight stitch P8-794
16. Van Dyke stitch P12-931
17. Whipped open chain stitch P8-841
18. Split stitch P8-841
19. Raised fishbone stitch leaf P8-640

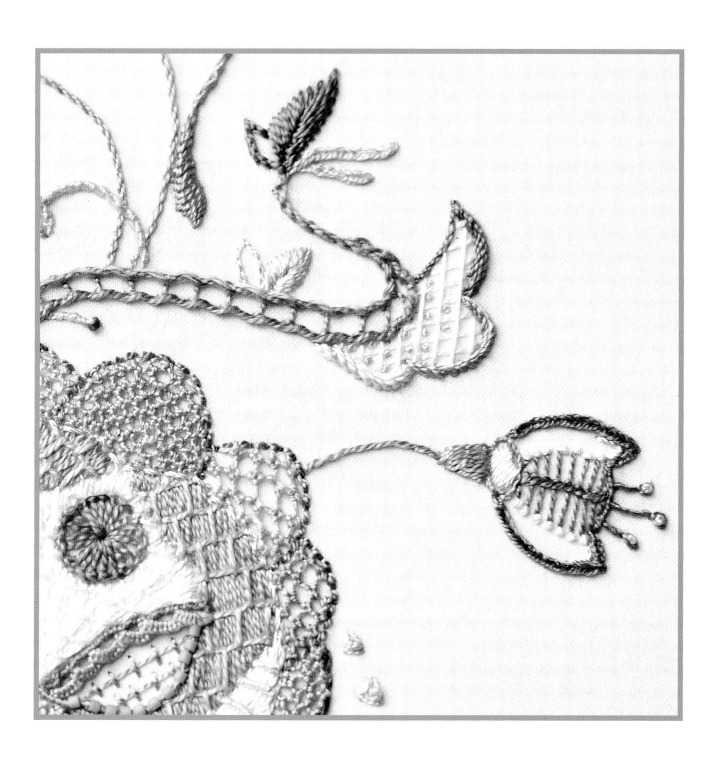

Zone 4: Textured bluebells

1. French knot P8-315; At-A
2. Portuguese knotted stem stitch P8-315
3. Whipped stem stitch P12-503
4. Backstitch At-A
5. Backstitch P8-794
6. Satin stitch At-A
7. Raised chain stitch band P8-959
8. French knot P8-3753
9. Whipped straight stitch P8-794
10. Raised chain stitch band P8-3753 + Woven filling P8-959
11. Raised stem stitch P12-503

12. Heavy chain stitch P12-778
13. French knot P12-503
14. Bullion knot P12-B5200
15. Raised stem stitch P12-503
16. Split stitch P8-794
17. Portuguese knotted stem stitch P8-794
18. Seed beads
19. Rope stitch P8-794
20. Stem stitch P12-503
21. Portuguese knotted stem stitch P8-3753

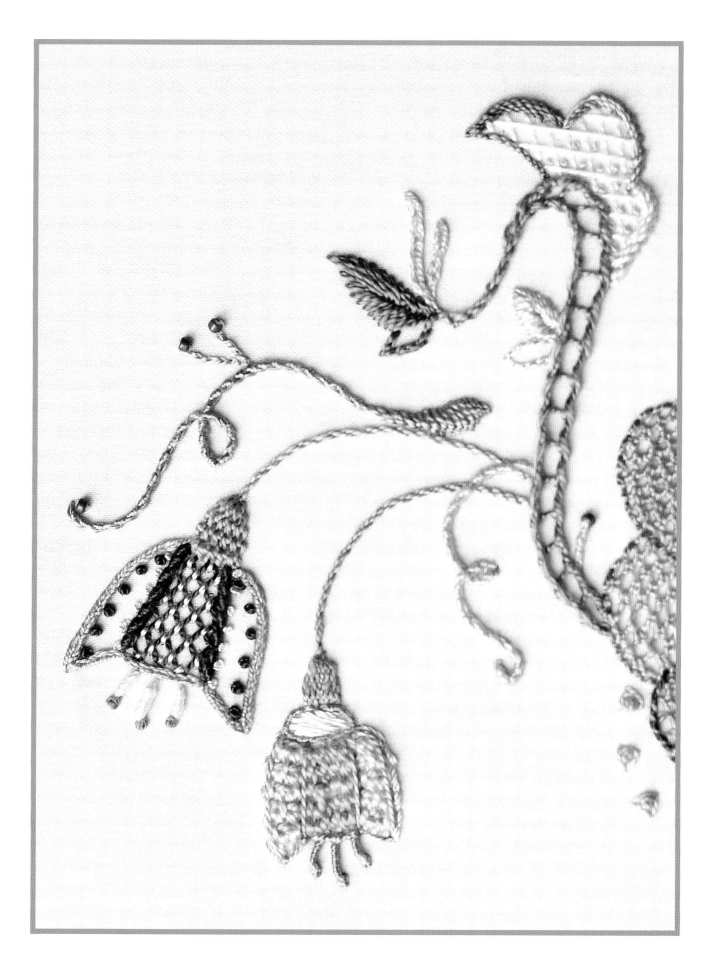

Scarlet Sails

This design is named after a popular Russian children's book by Alexander Grin. The heroine, Assol, lived in a small village with her father. She was only eight months old when her mother died of pneumonia. Her father was a seaman, and he had to leave his job to nurse his little daughter. To earn a living, he started making models of ships and selling them at fairs in the nearby town.

One day when Assol was eight years old, she was sent to the fair alone. One of the goods she needed to sell was a tiny yacht with sails of a very unusual colour: scarlet.

On her way to town, Assol had to go through a forest. There she noticed a small brook and could not resist trying out her favourite scarlet-sailed yacht in it. However, due to the current, the yacht soon sailed far away and Assol had to run after it. Eventually she found the yacht in the hands of an old storyteller, who prophesied that Assol's bridegroom would come to woo her sailing a ship with scarlet sails. The simple-hearted girl believed this prediction and told it to the people of her village, but they mocked her, thinking she must be half-witted.

Years later a young sea capitan came to the village and saw Assol. He was captivated by her beauty and asked people around to tell him all they knew about her. That is how he learned the story about the scarlet sails. He bought three thousand metres of scarlet silk and the very next morning Assol saw his scarlet-sailed ship coming to meet her, with musicians on board.

The two scarlet fire-buds, as they are called in this design, recall both the sails and the happy couple. Bells symbolize music and the undulating stems and leaves represent the waves of the sea.

Size: 13.5 x 16.5cm
(5¼ x 6½in)

Template: page 155

You will need

DMC PEARL COTTON THREAD SIZE 8:
SOLID COLOURS:
640 Beige grey – vy dk
642 Beige grey – dk
890 Pistachio green – ultra dk
938 Coffee brown – ultra dk

DMC PEARL COTTON THREAD SIZE 12:
SOLID COLOURS:
Ecru
666 Christmas red – bright
3033 Mocha brown – vy lt

DMC STRANDED COTTON THREAD
646 Beaver grey – dk
814 Garnet - dk
815 Garnet - med
816 Garnet
902 Garnet – vy dk
3053 Green grey
3705 Melon – dk

key

Pearl cotton thread size 8 is marked P8 in the instructions, e.g. 640 Beige grey is marked P8–640.

Pearl cotton thread size 12 is marked P12 in the instructions e.g. P12–666 is 666 Christmas red–bright pearl cotton thread size 12.

Stranded cotton thread is marked SC in the instructions, e.g. 814 Garnet – dk is marked SC–814.

The number in brackets means how many strands were used for the stitching e.g. SC–814 (1) means one strand.

For twisted cord, always take one strand and then fold it in half.

The five zones

1 RED FIRE-BUD

2 DOTTED FIRE-BUD

3 TOP TWIG

4 FRUIT CAPSULES

5 BELL AND LEAVES

Zone 1: Red fire bud

1. Silk shading SC-814; 815; 816; 902 (1)

2. Lattice P8-938 + SC-3053 (1) for couching

3. Portuguese knotted stem stitch P12-666

4. Fly stitch SC-814 (1)

5. French knot P8-642; 890

note

Please remember that the numbers allocated to each zone of the embroidery do not imply an order of stitching. The order in which you work is entirely up to you.

Zone 2: Dotted fire bud

1. Raised chain stitch band P8-640 + Woven filling P8-890

2. Split stitch P8-938

3. Woven filling (spaced bars) P8-938 (2)

4. Ceylon stitch SC-3705 (2)

5. Running stitch P8-938

6. French knot P12-666; SC-815; 902; 3705 (1)

7. Rope stitch SC-814 (2)

8. Whipped straight stitch SC-815 (1)

9. French knot SC-3053 (1)

10. Corded single Brussels stitch SC-902 (2)

11. Raised chain stitch band SC-815 (2)

12. Split stitch P8-640

13. Cretan stitch SC-646 (2)

Zone 3: Top twig

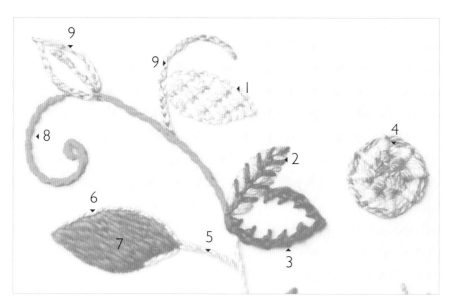

1. Lattice P12-Ecru + SC-3053 (2) for couching
2. Fly stitch leaf P8-938 + Straight stitch in between SC-3053 (3)
3. Palestrina stitch P8-938
4. Woven wheel P8-640; 642 + Ribbed spider web P12-Ecru
5. Portuguese knotted stem P12-3033
6. Backstitch P12-3033
7. Satin stitch P8-890
8. Portuguese knotted stem stitch P12-666
9. Split stitch P8-642

Zone 4: Fruit capsules

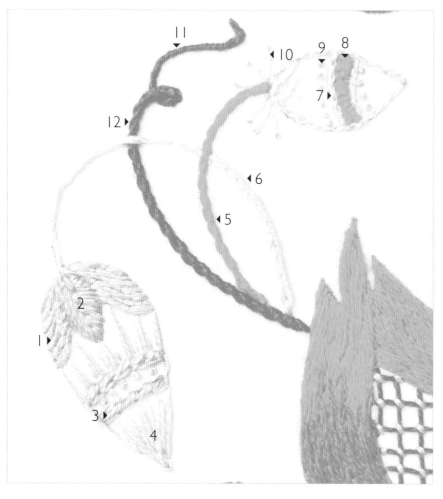

1. Satin stitch SC-3053 (2)
2. Fly stitch leaf SC-646 (2)
3. Chain stitch P8-640
4. Silk shading P12-Ecru; 3053 (1)
5. Portuguese knotted stem stitch P12-666
6. Heavy chain stitch P12-Ecru
7. Split stitch P12-Ecru
8. Heavy chain stitch P12-666
9. French knot P12-Ecru
10. Pistil stitch P12-Ecru
11. Split stitch P8-938
12. Portuguese knotted stem stitch P8-938

Zone 5: Bell and leaves

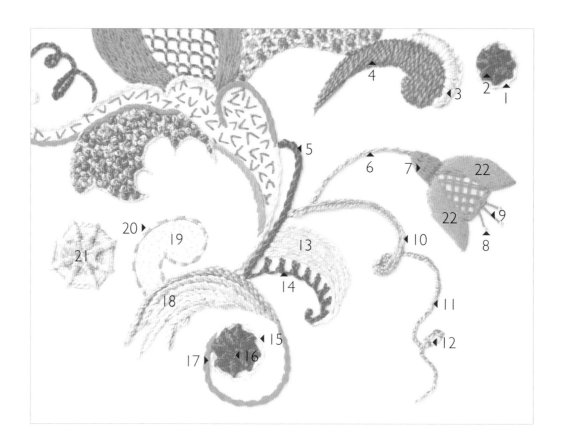

1. Split stitch P12-Ecru

2. Whipped wheel P8-938

3. Buttonhole stitch P12-Ecru + Straight stitches in between SC-3053 (2)

4. Satin stitch P8-890

5. Portuguese knotted stem stitch P8-938

6. Split stitch P8-642

7. Raised stem stitch SC-815 (2)

8. Whipped straight stitch SC-815 (2) + French knot SC-3053 (1)

9. Lattice SC-815 (2)

10. Heavy chain stitch P8-640

11. Rope stitch P8-640

12. Split stitch P8-640

13. Bokhara couching P12-3033 + SC-3053 (2) for couching

14. German knotted buttonhole stitch P8-938

15. Split stitch P12-Ecru

16. Ribbed spider web P8-938

17. Portuguese knotted stem stitch P12-666

18. Rope stitch, top to bottom: P8-640, P8-642, SC-3053 (2), P12-3033, P12-Ecru, SC-3053 (2), P8-642

19. Seeding SC-3053 (1)

20. Whipped running stitch SC-3053; 3705 (2)

21. Woven wheel P8-640; 642 + Ribbed spider web P12-Ecru

22. Raised stem stitch SC-3705 (2)

Crewel Waltz

This design was inspired by the widely known and dearly loved *Cinderella* by Charles Perrault. Its name represents the ball in the castle where all the magic started happening. Folk tales with a similar plot appear in the folklore of many different European peoples. For example, one of my favourites was *The Wild Strawberry,* a German fairy tale about a poor girl who used to gather berries in the forest so that she would have something to eat for her supper. One day she met an old woman suffering from hunger, and gave her all the berries she had gathered. In return for her kindness, this lady prophesied that good fortune would soon come her way.

Yellow, golden and purple shades dominate in this design: royal colours, with small additions of pale pink for tenderness. The one, two, three rhythm of the waltz dance step is figuratively shown in three intricate flower shapes circling together. There is a lot of lattice and openwork in this design to make it look lighter and to symbolize Cinderella's delicate wedding dress.

Crewel Waltz gives you plenty of opportunity to practise stitching techniques, as each of the elements is repeated three times.

Size: 20 x 20cm
(7⁷/₈ x 7⁷/₈in)

Template: page 156

You will need

DMC PEARL COTTON THREAD SIZE 8:

SOLID COLOURS:

211 Lavender – lt

208 Lavender – vy dk

725 Topaz

VARIEGATED:

90 Shades of yellow/orange

DMC PEARL COTTON THREAD SIZE 12:

SOLID COLOURS:

676 Old gold – lt

778 Antique mauve – vy lt

DMC STRANDED COTTON THREAD:

17 Yellow–green pear

30 Dark lilac – pale

444 Lemon – lt

554 Violet – lt

727 Topaz – vy lt

742 Tangerine – lt

745 Yellow – lt pale

746 Off-white

SEED BEADS:

15/0 Miyuki delica vy pale yellow

---

key

Pearl cotton thread size 8 is marked P8 in the instructions, e.g. 725 Topaz is marked P8–725.

Pearl cotton thread size 12 is marked P12 in the instructions e.g. P12–676 is 676 Old gold – lt Pearl cotton thread size 12.

Stranded cotton thread is marked SC in the instructions, e.g. 727 Topaz – vy lt is marked SC–727.

The number in brackets means how many strands were used for the stitching e.g. SC–727(1) means one strand.

For twisted cord always take one strand and then fold it in half.

The five zones

Each of these zones is repeated three times in the Crewel Waltz design. Taking this into consideration, I would recommend stitching similar areas all around the design first, before you go on to the next one. This will help to make all three flowers look very much alike.

1 DANCING FLOWER

2 LEFT LEAF

3 RIGHT LEAF

4 STEM

5 TENDRIL

Zone 1: Dancing flower

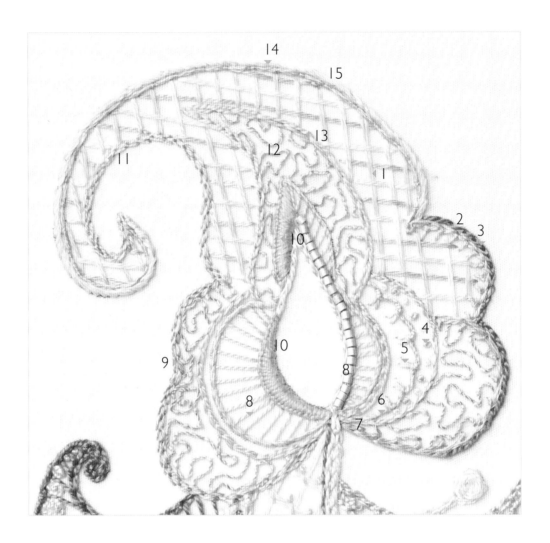

1. Lattice SC-727 (2) + Woven filling SC-30; 444 (2)

2. Mountmellick stitch SC-30 (2)

3. Split stitch P8-208

4. French knot SC-745 (1); P12-778

5. German knotted buttonhole stitch P12-778

6. Split stitch P12-778

7. Chain stitch P12-676

8. Whipped blanket stitch P12-676

9. Tuning fork stitch SC-30 (2)

10. Padded buttonhole stitch P12-676

11. Tuning fork stitch SC-554 (2)

12. Vermicelli stitch using twisted cord: SC-30 (1), couched with SC-17 (1)

13. Chain stitch P12-676

14. Rope stitch SC-17 (2)

15. Couching SC-554 (2) + (1) for couching

note

Please remember that the numbers allocated to each zone of the embroidery do not imply an order of stitching. The order in which you work is entirely up to you.

Zone 2: Left leaf

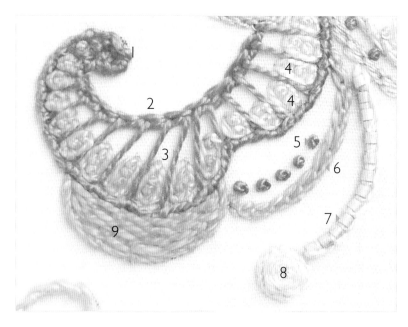

1. Rope stitch P8-208
2. Chain stitch P8-208
3. Whipped blanket stitch P8-208
4. Two French knots inside Lazy daisy stitch P8-90
5. French knot P8-208
6. Tuning fork stitch P8-90
7. Couched seed beads Miyuki delica 15/0
8. Woven wheel SC-746 (1)
9. Raised stem stitch P8-90

tip

For an optional, intricate finishing touch, a more interesting texture is created if the couched lines of seed beads in Zones 2 and 3 are worked over in Buttonhole stitch using two strands of pale yellow stranded cotton thread.

Zone 3: Right leaf

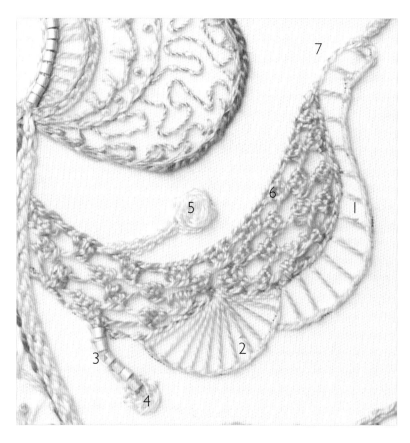

1. Whipped blanket stitch P12-676
2. Buttonhole scallop P12-676
3. Couched seed beads Miyuki delica 15/0
4. Woven wheel SC-17 (1)
5. Woven wheel SC-745 (1)
6. Brussels stitch 3+1 P12-778
7. Split stitch SC-17 (2)

Zone 4: Stem

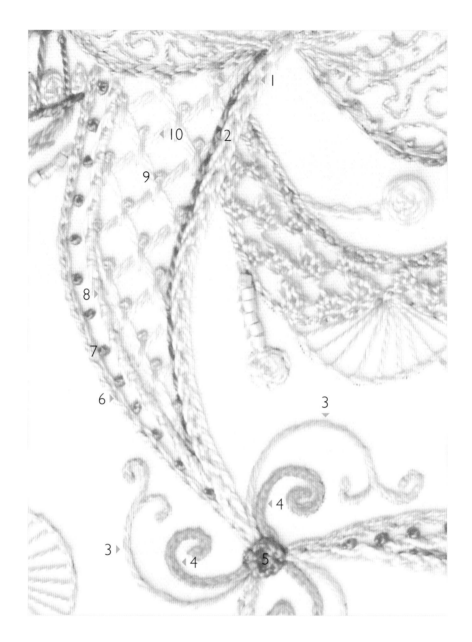

1. Hungarian braided chain stitch P8-211

2. Backstitch P8-208

3. Rope stitch P12-676

4. Chain stitch SC-742 (2)

5. Buttonhole wheel P8-208

6. Rope stitch SC-554 (For the two other stems, Chain stitch and Tuning fork stitch were used. You can do this or use Rope stitch for all three.)

7. French knot P8-208

8. Portuguese knotted stem stitch P8-211

9. Pistil stitch SC-742 (2)

10. Lattice SC-727 (3)

Zone 5: Tendril

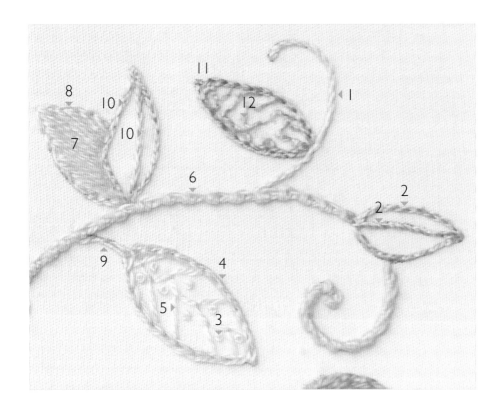

1. Stem stitch SC-17 (2)

2. Split stitch P12-778

3. French knot SC-746 (2)

4. Chain stitch SC-17 (2)

5. Feather stitch SC-746 (2)

6. Portuguese knotted stem stitch P8-725

7. Satin stitch SC-17 (2)

8. Split stitch SC-17 (2)

9. Whipped stem stitch SC-17 (2)

10. Split stitch P12-778

11. Chain stitch SC-30 (2)

12. Twisted cord: SC-30 (1) used for Vermicelli stitch; SC-17 (1) for couching

The owl's secret

First of all, why an owl? Once upon a time, long ago – around 2009 – my dearest brother gave me a troublesome birthday present: a personal website. At that time I had an embroidery hobby and 8-year-old twin boys, and unsurprisingly not a minute of free time! The first challenge was to think of a domain name for the website. Luckily I have my resourceful husband, who said: 'Since it's going to be an educational platform, why not use the owl, a bird associated with wisdom?' And so I named the website www.owl-crafts.com.

Civic Hall owl, Leeds.

Three years later at the Craft, Business & Hobby Show held in my native city of Kiev, I met an old Japanese friend of mine. By that time my first book, *Silk Ribbon and Embroidery* was published. He got very excited about the book and looked thoughtfully through it, asking how my embroidery business was going. When I told him about our domain name, he gave a sweet smile, then asked whether I knew that in Japanese tradition an owl is a symbol of good luck. I did not. And it was my turn to be surprised at his story, which sounded like a fairytale:

'In Japanese an owl is pronounced as *fukurou* or *fukuro*.

We give it poetic names: *Doctor of forest knowledge, Forest philosopher* and even *Forest ninja* because of its silent flight, swooping over its prey and ambushing in tree branches.'

The word *fukuro* can be spelled in three different ways. This is often the case in Japanese: different sets of hieroglyphs give the same sound and can form the same word, but the word gets a second, symbolic meaning. Written with one character, *fukuro* means just 'an owl', but written with two characters, it can mean 'no hardship or suffering', and written with three characters it means 'luck comes'.

Whether it is thanks to the lucky owl or not, I have been very fortunate in my work. Running the flower-themed embroidery business I always dreamed of truly gives me wings of happiness: lots of friends all round the globe, numerous travels and flowers, flowers, flowers all around me: stitched, photographed and live models for my future designs. Besides, stitching as a job is happiness in itself. In my house, there is no more nonsense like, 'Ask Mum, she's just stitching'. Instead it's: 'Shhh! Can't you see she's busy working?!'

It's no surprise that when it came to a brand name for my business, none of my family hesitated: Little Owl SmartCrafts ™ with the word 'art' hidden inside it. Because it is really all about crafts, but I always try to give it an artistic touch.

Leeds municipal owls.

I started collecting owl images: drawings, bags, sculptures, mugs, jewellery and more. My owl flock originates from all over the world: Japan, the USA, Turkey, Russia, Ukraine, Poland, Italy and China. I soon discovered that owls are popular in the UK too. It became almost impossible to work at my stand at the CHSI show in Birmingham, because friends kept asking whether I had seen the huge owl figure near the entrance, or the sweetest owlet postcard *ever* on sale nearby.

During a visit to one of the UK universities where my husband was working, I met a very sociable Vietnamese girl who insisted on taking me on a tour of the Owl City. She meant ancient Leeds, which has an Owl Trail of twenty-five owl figures placed in streets, squares and bridges all around the city. We did not have the Trail map and were short of time, so we often asked for help and the citizens were extremely kind, showing us the sights of their city. Thus we managed to take lot of photographs of the renowned owls of Leeds.

Right

A statue in an owl gown near a shopping centre in Leeds.

Ribbon Owl

Now to the next question: why ribbon? Needles and thread have been my best friends since my school days, but there was no room for ribbons in my soul at that time. Besides, I soon fell in love with floristry design and thought of nothing else but a career in that area. However, with one thing and another, my dream failed to come true. I almost fell into a deep depression as a result, though today it is clear to me that it all worked out for the best. Not long after, I discovered the silk ribbon embroidery technique and started designing flower bouquets stitched with silk ribbon. Soon my embroidery hobby turned into my main occupation and an integral part of my life.

My embroidery universe is divided into several lands: silk ribbon embroidery being one of them. Crewel and other kinds of thread embroidery such as silk shading seem like its rivals. Other rivals are soutache embroidery, micro-macramé jewellery making, needlelace techniques and more – but silk ribbon and the art of crewel stitching are the main contenders.

This is why I wanted to include this design: to celebrate the wonderful French art of stitching in silk ribbon, which amazingly turned one of the worst episodes in my life into a blessing. That is the real-life fairytale of my own, all bound up with flowers and happiness.

Of course, the 'You will need' list for Ribbon Owl design includes some natural silk ribbon. If you do not want to use this, replace it with silk shading for example, and attach a nice little button to the owl's hat instead of the ribbon rose.

You can make the finished piece an embroidered wall-hanging, a pillowcase, an appliqué design for an apron or a cover for a jewellery box. I made it with a tote bag in mind. If you want to work on this idea, you can use either a plain fabric in any nice pale colour or a patterned one, as shown in these instructions. You will find tips on transferring a design onto patterned fabric on page 144.

Size: 21.6 x 18.4cm
(8½ x 7¼in)

Template: page 157

You will need

DMC PEARL COTTON THREAD SIZE 8:

VARIEGATED:

105 Shades of brown

125 Shades of seafoam green

DMC PEARL COTTON THREAD SIZE 12:

SOLID COLOURS:

503 Blue green – med

712 Cream

822 Beige grey – lt

842 Beige brown – vy lt

3033 Bocha brown – vy lt

3813 Blue green – lt

3823 Yellow – ultra pale

DMC STRANDED COTTON THREAD:

309 Rose – dk

761 Salmon – lt

772 Yellow green – vy lt

967 Apricot – vy lt

989 Forest green

3053 Green grey

3345 Hunter green – dk

3346 Hunter green

3823 Yellow – ultra pale

NATURAL SILK RIBBON:

7mm V241 Seafoam green, variegated

key

Pearl cotton thread size 8 is marked P8 in the instructions, e.g. 125 Shades of seafoam green is marked P8–125.

Pearl cotton thread size 12 is marked P12 in the instructions e.g. P12–503.

Stranded cotton thread is marked wSC in the instructions, e.g. 309 Rose – dk is marked SC–309.

The number in brackets means how many strands were used for the stitching e.g. SC–309 (1) means one strand.

For twisted cord always take one strand and then fold it in half.

Transferring the design

Besides the usual ways of transferring a design – see page 9 for my favourites – there is this one for patterned fabrics. For this I use water soluble fabric stabilizer. It is a popular soluble backing for sewing as well as for free machine embroidery. There are dozens of manufacturers, but my favourite is Soluvlies by Vilene, produced in Germany. Using water soluble fabric marker, I transfer patterns onto Soluvlies and than attach it on top of my embroidery fabric.

The four zones

1 OWL

2 FLOWERS ON THE HAT

3 BOW, LEFT SIDE

4 BOW, RIGHT SIDE

Zone 1: Owl

You may have heard of a Lark's head knot, which is very popular in macramé. For the owl design we are going to work Lark's head scallops using this very knot (see page 30 in the Stitch guide). You just need to know two macramé terms before we start: 1) knotting cord, which means the cord(s) used to make knots; and 2) knot-bearing cord, which is the one that supports the knots.

Please bear in mind that the photograph on page 30 shows a rope used for the knot-bearing cord. However, here we need a different base for a scallop: work a loose Lazy daisy stitch the size of a scallop (one stitch for a scallop is enough) and then tie Lark's head knots using the two threads of the Lazy daisy stitch as the knot-bearing cord.

note

Please remember that the numbers allocated to each zone of the embroidery do not imply an order of stitching. The order in which you work is entirely up to you.

1.   Silk ribbon 7mm silk ribbon V-241

2.   Rope stitch P8-105

3.   Romanian stitch + Straight stitch P12-712; 822; 842

4.   Straight stitch P12-712

5.   Straight stitch P8-105

6.   Basket stitch P8-105

7.   Battlement couching P12-712; 822; 842; 3033

8.   Lark's head scallops P8-105

9.   Raised stem stitch P8-105

10. Buttonhole wheel P12-3813

11. Pistil stitch P12-3813

12. Stem stitch P12-3033

13. Stem stitch 7mm silk ribbon V-241

14. Raised stem stitch P12-3813

15. Rope stitch P12-503

16. Ribbon rose 7mm silk ribbon V-241

Zone 2: Flowers on the hat

1. Padded buttonhole stitch SC-309 (2); (1)
2. French knot SC-967 (1)
3. Straight stitch + Lazy daisy stitch SC-761 (1)
4. Satin stitch SC-3346 (2)
5. Twisted cord SC-3345 (1)
6. Twisted cord in two rows SC-3345; 3346 (1)
7. Padded buttonhole stitch SC-967 (3); (1)
8. French knot SC-309 (1)
9. Straight stitch + Lazy daisy stitch SC-761 (1)
10. Satin stitch SC-3345 (2)
11. Twisted cord SC-3346 (1)
12. Twisted cord SC-3053 (1)
13. Padded buttonhole stitch SC-3346 (2); (1)
14. Padded buttonhole stitch SC-3053 (3); (1)

Zone 3: Bow. left side

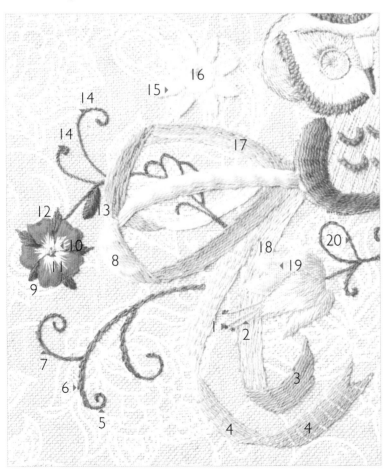

1. Straight stitch SC-3345 (1)
2. Twisted cord SC-3053 (1)
3. Raised stem stitch P8-125
4. Bokhara couching P8-125
5. Stem stitch SC-3345 (2)
6. Tuning fork stitch SC-3346 (2)
7. Stem stitch SC-3345 (2)
8. Raised stem stitch P8-125
9. Satin stitch SC-3346 (2)
10. Straight stitch SC-761 (1)
11. French knot SC-761; 3346 (1)
12. Padded buttonhole stitch SC-309 (3); (1)
13. Raised fishbone stitch leaf SC-3345 (2)
14. Twisted cord SC-3346 (1)
15. Picot stitch P12-3823
16. Woven wheel SC-3823 (2)
17. Alternate stem stitch P8-125
18. Stem stitch P12-3813
19. Padded buttonhole stitch SC-967 (3); (1)
20. Stem stitch SC-3345 (2)

STITCHING FLOWER PETALS IN ZONES 2 AND 3

1   2   3   4

Key

1 *Flower petal outlines*

2 *Padding*

3 *Buttonhole stitch worked over the padding*

4 *Lazy daisy stitches (shown in green) alternating with Straight stitches (yellow lines)*

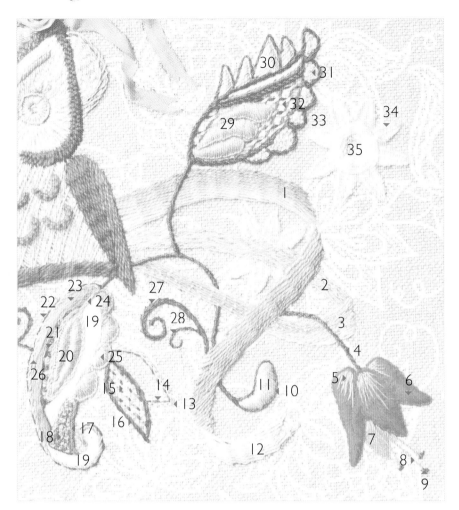

1. Raised stem stitch P8-125

2. Alternate stem stitch P12-3813

3. Bokhara couching P8-125; P12-3813

4. Twisted cord SC-3346 (1)

5. Straight stitch SC-761 (1)

6. Padded buttonhole stitch SC-309 (3); (1)

7. Padded buttonhole stitch SC-761 (2); (1)

8. Twisted cord SC-3053 (1)

9. Straight stitch SC-3345 (1)

10. Stem stitch SC-3346 (1)

11. Padded satin stitch SC-722 (2); (1)

12. Padded raised stem stitch P8-125

13. Chain stitch SC-3053 (2)

14. Backstitch SC-3346 (2)

15. Lattice SC-772; 3346 (2)

16. Rope stitch SC-3345 (2)

17. Rope stitch SC-3346 (2)

18. French knot SC-772; 3346 (2)

19. Woven filling (spaced bars) SC-3823 (2)

20. Padded buttonhole stitch SC-3053 (3); (1)

21. French knot SC-772; 3346 (1)

22. Running stitch SC-3345 (2)

23. Woven filling (spaced bars) SC-989 (2)

24. Twisted cord SC-772 (1)

25. Padded buttonhole scallops SC-772 (2); (1)

26. Twisted cord SC-772 (1)

27. Chain stitch SC-3346 (2)

28. Stem stitch SC-3346 (1)

29. Padded buttonhole stitch SC-3053 (3); (1)

30. Padded buttonhole stitch SC-772 (3); (1)

31. French knot SC-772 (1)

32. Lattice SC-3346; 772 (2)

33. Stem stitch SC-3346 (1)

34. Picot stitch P12-3823

35. Woven wheel SC-3823 (3)

note: for stitch number 9

Rather than the usual French knots, two or three Straight stitches were used to suggest the anthers of a lily.

Patterns

TREE OF HAPPINESS

See page 52. Shown at half original size.
Enlarge to 200% before transferring.

EMERALD CITY

See page 94. Shown full size.

RIBBON OWL

See page 143. Shown full size.

Stitch index

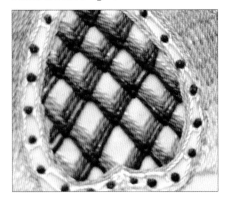

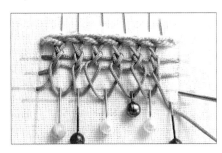

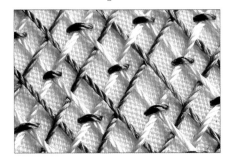

Bibliography

Encyclopedia of Needlework, Thérèse de Dillmont,
Bracken Books, new edition 1987
Encyclopedia of Victorian Needlework, Sophia Frances
Anne Caulfeild, Dover Publications, 1972
Three-Dimensional Embroidery Stitches, Pat Trott,
Search Press, 2005
Crewel Twists, Hazel Blomkamp, Search Press, 2012
Jacobean Crewel Work and Traditional Designs,
Penelope, Wm. Briggs & Co, 1950